I 'Ate You Butler!
The Making of On the Buses

Just because there's snow on the roof,
doesn't mean the fire's gone out...

I 'Ate You Butler!
The Making of On the Buses

Tex Fisher
with Ronald Wolfe & Ronald Chesney

Deck Chair Publishing

First published in Great Britain in 2011 by
Deck Chair Publishing
www.deckchairpublishing.co.uk

1

Limited Edition Number:

ISBN-13: 978-0956563415

Printed and Bound by CPI Antony Rowe, Chippenham

Cover Design: Tex Fisher
Images: Jeanne Varney, Anna Karen, Alan Hunter-Craig, Tony
Young, David Dederick, Avril Gaynor, Tex Fisher, Onthebuses.net

Set in Calibri and Cooper Std

Contents:

Acknowledgments

Hearing the story of *On the Buses* from the people involved was the vital key to this book working, so my sincere thanks goes out to everybody who has helped to make that ambition a reality.

Firstly, I am indebted to Ronald Chesney and Ronald and Rose Wolfe, for offering their valuable time to this project. I spent many happy hours chatting to them at BAFTA in London, so my gratitude extends to them for being so hospitable.

Additional thanks go to Anna Karen, the stupendous Olive, who kindly offered her time for a natter about her work on the series, as well as Anna's close friend and colleague, Kate Williams, who generously assisted my research with an interview.

Thanks also to directors Howard Ross and Derrick Goodwin, designer Alan Hunter-Craig, sound supervisor Paul Faraday, composer Geoff Unwin, writers Jonathan Lynn and George Layton, Michelle Monro, Avril Gaynor, and Michael Grade. My thanks also goes to the late Christopher Neame, a producer at Hammer, who sadly died just weeks before this book was published. My additional thanks to Reg Varney's daughter Jeanne, and Michael Robbins' widow, Hal Dyer. As well as Ursula Mohan, Patricia Clapton, Linda Regan, Derek Carpenter, Laura Graham, Carolae Donaghue. I also have to thank Dario at Pontins at Prestatyn, with additional kudos to Tony and Ann Young who helped with their recollections and images.

My thanks are also extended to the fans of this show, most notably Rob Reel who runs the Official On the Buses Facebook fan page. I also have to thank the consortium at the Official On the Buses Appreciation Society and Forums who own Reg Varney's diaries, for allowing me to sneak a peek, and reproduce a few extracts in the book. Thanks also to Scott, Nick, Geoff at CPI, and Christine and David their support. Last but not least, endless thanks to Paul Donnelley for his tireless work in improving my atrocious grammar.

I would also like to thank Stephen Lewis, who, despite declining all attempts to be interviewed for this book, remains a hero of mine.

Introduction

Ah...*On the Buses*. That wonderful product of 1970s Britain: bawdy, brash, full of big knockers and flashed knickers, filthy laughs, pinched fish and chips, and tall Hitler-esque figures getting splashed with water - what more could the viewer ask for?

I was first introduced to *On the Buses* on Christmas Day, in 1997. I was only 6-years-old at the time, but I was captivated as ITV repeated the three *On the Buses* feature films as part of its Christmas line-up.

At first, I didn't get the jokes but the buses enthralled me. As a child, I loved buses, and I seemed to be at the London Transport Museum almost weekly, as sad as it may sound. I remember a shelf in my room collapsed one day because of the amount of Corgi models it contained. I was so fond of buses. To have them beamed into my living room was viewing heaven.

Since then, my tastes and hobbies matured, as did my television viewing choices and, as I grew older and expanded my repertoire of period classics, I started to understand the saucy humour, the double entendres, and what Turnaround Betty really meant when she was taking Jack upstairs.

With the advent of the Granada Plus satellite channel, I was able to watch these classics a lot more frequently. I started to annoy people by quoting lines verbatim, going up to people and saying, "What a lot of rot you do talk." My re-enactments were seldom appreciated, and it was quite a mistake for whoever bought me the full series and the three films on video for a birthday present when I was about eleven.

I continued to watch the shows, upgraded my collection to DVD, and remained a devoted fan of the programmes. In my teens, I indulged in buying some additional memorabilia for the shows, getting a few film posters, a fair few vintage Look-In magazines, and snippets of interviews with the cast and writers in the *TV Times*. I usually tried to conceal such purchases from my friends, and hide the fact I was an admirer of a programme a good twenty years older than myself, but now, thirteen years since I first sampled this classic show, I'm proud to call myself an *On the Buses* fan.

To be given the chance to write this book by the prolific scribes, Ronald Wolfe and Ronald Chesney, was an incredible opportunity. I leapt at being able to compile it, chat to the cast, their relatives, and many of the people who worked on the programme.

I, like all other fans, know the episodes backwards, and can quote lines ad nauseam, but to this day, I have found the story of how the show came about seems to be hushed up. There is a book, many fan clubs, and many websites - all devoted to this wonderful show, but nobody has bothered to dig a little deeper into the programme and peek behind the depot doors.

So, forty-one years late - here is that story.

Now get that bus out!

Tex Fisher, London, England
October 2010

From Rag Trade to Riches

When a 17-year-old Rene Cadier topped the bill of local variety theatres in the early 1940s, people could be forgiven for
not realising that the musical prodigy, playing Chopin's classics
on the harmonica with perfect harmony, would go on to co-
write one of the most popular situation comedies of all time.
Rene Cadier didn't see the change coming either. "I started
playing the Harmonica at sixteen", he recalled. "Somebody
had given me the instrument, much to my father's annoyance, and I learnt to play it, and became rather good. I went
along to a music shop, and the vendor said I should go on
stage. In those days, the local cinemas had live theatre shows
in between the films, and I made my debut in one of those."

As Rene developed his musical talents, the venues became
larger and more substantial, and he realised that his French
birth name would need to be simplified to stick in the memories of his audience. Taking inspiration from the variety act Flanagan and Allen, he renamed himself Ronald Chesney. "I was
born in England, but my parents were both French," Ronald explained. "I learnt rather quickly that nobody could pronounce
my surname, so I changed it to Chesney. I had been working
with Bud Flanagan and Chesney Allen, so took it from there."

With a new stage identity, the possibilities of career pro-
gression became limitless, and Chesney continued to build

on his musical work. From an initial spot on BBC Radio programme *Palace of Varieties*, he gained his own show, entertaining the troops throughout the Second World War. "I had a kidney removed so couldn't serve, but I played harmonica on the radio," Chesney remembered. "I had thousands of letters from all around the world, from troops out in the desert wanting to play harmonica, it was incredible. I suppose in the desert there is little else to do!"

The harmonica playing continued, with impressive performances in South Africa, France and Australia, and on his return to Britain, appearances at the London Palladium; on the same bill as Laurel and Hardy, and a two-hour recital at the Royal Albert Hall, playing to audiences of more than five thousand.

After more than ten years as a musician, and highly regarded for his talents, Chesney's decision to retire from his music was an unexpected one. It came in the mid-1950s, when he, along with several other solo musicians, were given a place on the radio programme *Educating Archie.* The radio programme, based around an ventriloquist, became a popular show, and offered a further channel for Ronald's musical performances. "The show had three sketches, and in between those sketches they had three spots for music. I was playing in one of them, and in another there was a young girl singing. It was Julie Andrews!"

Educating Archie introduced the listener to an extensive gallery of comedic talent including, Max Bygraves, Tony Hancock, Benny Hill, Dick Emery, Bruce Forsyth and Warren Mitchell. Comedienne Beryl Reid also joined the show, and brought along her long-time scriptwriter, Ronald Wolfe.

Wolfe had been Beryl's scriptwriter for more than ten years, and when she joined *Educating Archie*, he made the move with her, contributing sketches to the programme, and eventually becoming head scriptwriter after Eric Sykes left the team to work on other shows.

Educating Archie went on to tour Australia, and impressed audiences so much that the television company ABC commissioned a full series. In urgent need of additional material, Ronald Wolfe joined Ronald Chesney to write more episodes, and the harmonica playing diminished as the writing progressed. "I didn't want to be a musician for the rest of my life," Chesney explained. "So I started writing more with Ronald Wolfe and Marty Feldman." When Marty Feldman decided to move on to pastures new, Wolfe and Chesney remained as writing partners and, back in England, continued to script radio comedy, writing episodes of Sid James's programme *It's a Deal*, before deciding to create a series of their own. "It seemed clear that the future was in television, so we came up a series called with *The Rag Trade*."

Basing their work on previous experience was a key factor and, thankfully, both Wolfe and Chesney had strong ideas to contribute. "I had worked in the Marconi radio factory during the Second World War," Wolfe recalled. "It was from there I learnt about the unions, and the shop stewards." Ronald Chesney's parents had been in the garment business. "Being both French, they worked in the silk trade," explained Chesney. "I learnt a lot about dress-making from there. We brought our ideas together, and used them to develop the show. It worked well because our experiences could be put quite neatly together."

There were many tales of workers taking against the boss from Wolfe's time at the radio factory that made it to the screen in *The Rag Trade*. Squirting glue into the time clock to slow it down, nominating a select couple who would clock-in everybody else before they actually arrived, and even clocking in for the night shift at 8 o'clock in the evening, going home, returning at 6am, clocking out, and pretending they'd been there all night.

The workers also skived off with lengthy toilet breaks, loitering in the cubicles to smoke and chat, all during working hours. When the management had the cheek to time the workers' toilet breaks, the foreman would call a lightning strike. The foreman became Paddy, the management became Mr Fenner, and the radio factory transformed into Fenner Fashions. Ronald Wolfe's brief stint at the electrical company became the idea behind *The Rag Trade*. "We took the idea to one of the independent companies, but they weren't too keen," Chesney explained "They said that most of the country worked at a factory, and wouldn't want to watch a factory when the got home."

Thankfully, an old acquaintance of the pair, Frank Muir, had recently been appointed at the BBC as a comedy advisor with Denis Norden. After pitching their idea to him, Wolfe and Chesney landed their first major television series, one which would become a huge success.

"The BBC had thirty-nine episodes, then we revived it in

The Reg Trade

As an all-round performer, Reg Varney contributed his own dash of humour to his acting work, and developed the scripted situations further to gain more laughs. One such instance of this was in the first series of *The Rag Trade* in 1962. Varney was required to eat two eggs at once, but to further exploit humour potential, he stuck together two spoons to make a 'double egg spoon'.

As June Whitfield explained on Reg Varney's *This is Your Life* in 1971, the BBC had many letters from viewers enquiring where they could purchase Varney's invention, but it never went into production.

1978 on LWT with another twenty-two episodes," Wolfe explained. "We had learnt the first lesson in comedy, always know the subject!"

The main star of *The Rag Trade* was militant female shop steward Paddy Fleming, played by the late Miriam Karlin, and the show also featured Esma Cannon, Shirley Hancock and Peter Jones as Mr Fenner. But the programme required an additional dash of talent. The head cutter, Reg Turner, was still to be cast. Eventually, this part was awarded to variety performer Reg Varney. "I first met Reg Varney in Bournemouth," explained Ronald Chesney. "I was in the theatre there, playing the harmonica, and he was on the same bill. I could see he was very talented, so I suggested him for *The Rag Trade*. As we know, he later became Stan in *On the Buses*."

With Fenner Fashions quickly becoming a household name, *The Rag Trade* harvested impressive viewing figures, firmly setting the reputations of its writers and stars, and also scoring success in Australia. "Miriam Karlin was invited to do a show in Australia on the back of the series," recalled Ronald Chesney. "She was Jewish, and Ronald Wolfe is Jewish, so she tended to speak to him more than me, but I remember she enquired, 'I suppose I'll have to take my bleeding whistle,' and Ronnie said she may as well. But when Miriam arrived in Australia it was a Jewish holiday, so she was invited to the Sydney chief synagogue. After the service, the rabbi said, 'Thank you all for coming, and it only remains for me to ask our honoured guest Miss Miriam Karlin to blow her whistle and shout "'Ev'rybody Out!"' That's a true story!"

When *The Rag Trade* came to an end, Ronald Wolfe and Ronald Chesney did some writing for the theatre, most notably rewriting and developing a stage show in Blackpool, working with Thora Hird and Freddie Frinton. The writers were impressed with the talents of the duo and, with a new idea for a television sitcom brewing, Wolfe and Chesney devised a second series for the BBC, entitled *Meet The Wife*, creating the programme specifically with Hird and Finton in mind. *Meet the Wife* ran from 1963 until 1966, being sold to the BBC from an initial pilot of the long-running *Comedy Playhouse* series. "The pilot episode was an incredible success," Chesney remembers. "It was number one in all the ratings, and was one of the most successful programme of the *Comedy Playhouse* series."

From the initial success of the *Comedy Playhouse* episode, *Meet the Wife* was made into a full series on the BBC, be it rather reluctantly by the powers at be. "The BBC weren't too keen to make the full series, they weren't keen on Thora and Freddie, saying things like 'What on earth do you want to use those clapped out has-beens for?', but they felt they owed us a favour after *The Rag Trade* had become such a success. So we did a full series, and it was another great success!"

In 1968, another *Comedy Playhouse* episode was scripted entitled *Wild, Wild Women.* This little known show had a similar plot to *The Rag Trade,* but it was set in the early 1900s. The pilot led to a series starring Barbara Windsor, a background character from *The Rag Trade* but ran for just seven episodes. Whilst in production, the writers were already feverishly devising another laugh-a-minute sitcom. This time it would be set in a bus depot.

- 2 -

Get That Bus Out!

Introduction

A total of thirty-five hours of *On the Buses* were created over the magical five-year timescale from 1969 to 1973. Both adored and panned in equal measure, the ribald series tickled the nation's ribs and caused ripples of irritation among the more miserable critics who cast the series as their principal bête noire.

The comedy followed the life of the skirt-chasing bus driver Stan Butler and his work at the dysfunctional Luxton & District Traction Company, together with conductor best mate Jack Harper and petty martinet Inspector Cyril 'Blakey' Blake. When the turmoil of the working day was over, Stan would retire home to be greeted by his overbearing mother, dowdy, bespectacled sister Olive and her indolent husband. Life was seldom smooth in Luxton.

With upwards of sixteen million viewers tuning in during the show's prime, *On the Buses* swiftly became a staple of

I 'Ate You Butler! - The Making of On the Buses

British television, and even spawnded three cinematic films. The first in 1971, also entitled *On the Buses*, out-grossed both *James Bond* and *Get Carter* combined. An indisputable legend in British cultural history, *On the Buses* became a globally popular series, having been sold in more than thirty-five countries and making its stars heavily in-demand personalities.

Having remained popular for an astonishing forty years, with its own series in America and constant reruns in prime-time slots around the world, *On the Buses* maintains its position in the top echelon of the most influential and memorable television series of all time.

The Idea

It was the late 1960s, and having already gained significant success with several classic sitcoms earlier in the decade, Ronald Wolfe and Ronald Chesney were looking for a new idea for a situation comedy. "We didn't really have an idea of what we wanted to do yet," explains Ronald Chesney. "All we knew was that we wanted to use Reg Varney again, as he had been very good to us in *The Rag Trade*."

"We went through several lines of thought," Ronald Wolfe explains. "Firstly, we knew we wanted Reg in the lead. We then thought what this character would do for a living - a shopkeeper, a plumber, an electrician?" After a few preliminary ideas, it appeared that one situation stood from out the others. Wolfe and Chesney had no reservations in singling out a setting, seeing humour in the everyday life of a bus driver. Whereas many budding writers would see a bus, a depot and a bus inspector as little potential for comedy, Wolfe and Chesney were adamant that there was significant leeway in scoring laughs from it, and knew from their previous experience that the audiences like something they could relate to in television comedy.

"Everything just seemed to fit around a bus driver," Ronald Chesney recalled. "Both myself and Ronnie Wolfe had already devised two shows for the BBC; *The Rag Trade* and *Meet the Wife*. The first had been about a dress factory and the other was based in a working-class home. We were keen to put together a combination of both work and home and decided to do buses, as we could have Stan at the depot, and then back at home. It was a great opportunity to bring to the two series together, and I don't know many other shows that have those two separations in setting. Buses worked with everything, and it also related to the audience. When somebody sees a bus-man's uniform, they already know a lot about him."

Wolfe and Chesney were correct with their logic. See a bus driver and you instantly know what he does for a job, you know he drives people about, has a conductor on board with him, and an inspector back at the depot. However, the formula to base comedy on a recognisable situation could have related to many occupations. A postman, a train driver, a dentist; all offer some immediate familiarity of the job role and could have equally been exploited for comedic purposes, but for Wolfe and Chesney, it had to be buses. "We wanted an Inspector to worry him at work," explained Ronald Chesney, "and we wanted a conductor to go along on the bus with him and get up to no good - for us, all the things we wanted from our characters just seemed to fit around working at a bus depot, so that's how we ended up with *On the Buses*."

Developing the Format

Developing the initial plan was the next cog in the process, and Wolfe and Chesney delighted in thinking of all the problems they could burden on poor Stan. "We wanted to make his life a misery at work," Chesney laughs. "We knew the Inspector would see to that. The most important thing all along was conflict. It is bland and boring without some spark of anguish between the characters. So, to get some more conflict, we also made sure Stan was single, we thought there was more fun in that idea, as he could always be after the girls."

"Where he lived was our next question. Again, we were keen to put troubles in the way of Stan, so we put him at home with his possessive mother. We also needed someone in the house for him to clash with. He was a pleasant chap so couldn't argue too much with his mother, but he could with his sister Olive and brother-in-law, Arthur, so we put them in the house too!"

Would the Idea Work?

"All ideas needed to be tested," recalls Ronald Wolfe. "So we, of course, had to do the same with *On the Buses*." This was the stage that everything could fall apart at the seams. Should the plan not have enough potential, then it could go no further. The method of testing was simple - think up some episode ideas. "We had learnt this was the best strength test," Wolfe continued. "If we could think of ideas for the first six episodes, then we could assume that the formula may work. We were rather confident in the idea after that."

Commissioning

"It didn't take us long to sketch a few plans together," remembers Ronald Chesney. "We had jotted down our ideas and decided to take it to the BBC, who had been very good to us in the past with our earlier comedies. Michael Mills was the Head of Comedy, and he didn't like it". Despite having a strong plan for their new programme, together with a water-tight list of possible actors to play the parts, the road down to the Cemetery Gates was far from clear. "The head of light entertainment at the BBC just couldn't see the merit, he was never a friend of ours" Chesney recalls. "He just said "'So the bus comes in late, there's oil on the depot floor, what else?'" He couldn't see the domestic side of the sitcom, with Stan's family at home."

This negativity was a weakening blow to Wolfe and Chesney's brainchild, but they were a long way from giving up on the series. The newly formed London Weekend Television had its doors wide open, and with an old friend as head of light entertainment, Wolfe and Chesney tried their luck. "Frank Muir was a good friend of ours and we took it to him less than a week after the BBC rejected us. Frank knew us, knew our work, and knew we could sustain a whole series so we had a good chance," Ronald Chesney confirmed.

Muir, along with his colleague Denis Norden, had once been assistant Head of Light Entertainment at the BBC, and had helped with Wolfe and Chesney's first sitcom, *The Rag Trade*, making it to the screen. Now, with Muir in charge of entertainment at the newly formed London Weekend Television, there was a chance to sneak the idea in through the back door. Ronald Wolfe and Ronald Chesney pitched him *On the Buses*. A last chance of rescuing the show from the waste paper basket was offered to the duo, and thankfully, Frank Muir gave them the green light."

Within about five minutes, Frank had been on the phone to Cyril Bennett, the programme controller, who had cleared the idea, and came back with the response "LWT has got itself a bus company!" It was a sudden decision, but one that LWT would never regret.

"There was a genuine interest in the securing the show for LWT on Frank's part," explained assistant director Howard Ross. "It was initially seen as downmarket comedy, but it was popularist. It's all about audience and profit at the end of the day. But Frank knew the writers, and he knew Reg, and the package of the show came with Reg in it. I wasn't at the first meeting with Frank and the writers, but Frank would have just commissioned it, and then found a producer for it."

Choosing a Producer

When it came to choosing a producer for *On the Buses*, Frank Muir knew the perfect person. "The plans were starting to fall into place, and both of us could visualise the end result," Ronald Chesney recalled. "The next thing we needed to do was get a producer for the show and we ended up with Stuart Allen, who had just come from *All Gas and Gaiters*. Frank Muir suggested him, and we met up with one another, and he was delighted to be part of it all."

"Stuart Allen was a very good director," explained director Howard Ross. "He'd been at the BBC before, and I worked with him on LWT's very first show, which was *Never a Cross Word*. Ours was actually meant to be the second programme aired, but there was a technical problem and we broadcast first. I assisted Stuart on many productions, and directed some *On the Buses* episodes myself."

Allen directed thirty-eight episodes of *On the Buses,* before he handed over the reins to other directors in 1971, Derrick Goodwin, Howard Ross and Brian Izzard.

"I don't know why Stuart called it a day," Goodwin explained. "All I know was I got a call from LWT to see if I could take it over in 1971. I had been writing and producing a show with Rodney Bewes, which was quite successful, so they thought I should do *On the Buses*. Cyril Bennett, who was programme controller, said that if I did *On the Buses*, I could do something that I wanted to do afterwards. So I went to meet the writers and the cast, and took over for eighteen episodes."

Casting

"This was by far our hardest challenge, but I think we got it just right," Ronald Wolfe explained triumphantly. The writers knew from their previous work that correctly casting the characters was the true secret to success. If they could find a spark of divine intervention to choose the right six actors, who would blend harmoniously together and were agreeable to the viewers, they would surely have a hit formula.

Reg Varney, an experienced variety performer and star of Wolfe and Chesney's *The Rag Trade* some six years earlier, was the first choice for Stan Butler. "He had been our foreman in *The Rag Trade*, and we knew that his superb experience and charisma would make him a wonderful Stan," Chesney explained. "But Reg was in Australia at the time, so we weren't sure if he could be in the show. We sent him some details of our idea, and thankfully he was more than happy to do it. I remember the wire we got from him - it just said, 'Right, I'm learning to drive a bus!'"

Although Reg Varney was first choice as Stan, on the list of possible actors presented to Frank Muir, he was placed second, nestled between Ronnie Barker and Bernard Cribbins. "He was always going to be our Stan," Wolfe confirmed. "But we had learnt that the executives seldom agree with the writer's choice of casting. They treat the list like a wine list, they tend to go for the second because it seems safer." But if luck turned against them, and Ronnie Barker was selected by the executive producer to be Stan, would Wolfe and Chesney be pleased? "Not really!" Chesney explained. "Ronnie was a great actor, but he was a character actor. He always played someone else, whereas Reg just played himself. I'm glad we got Varney. He wasn't very good at the first script read-through, but by the time he had taken it home, he came back and he had learnt not only his part, but also everybody else's. He was the star, but he was very down to earth."

Reg was delighted to be offered the job, and was sure the show had potential. "Dad thought it would be a safe bet as it had both work and home life combined," Varney's daughter, Jeanne, explained. "It had the contrast that could give rise to many funny situations. He was thrilled to be working with the Ronnies again, as he had done *The Rag Trade*. He considered them to be excellent writers."

With Stan cast, the attentions turned to Inspector Blake. Actor Dudley Foster was the original suggestion for Blakey. "We sent Dudley's agent a script, and heard nothing back," recalls Ronald Wolfe. "But he was unavailable for some reason, and a few years later he committed suicide." Director Stuart Allen instead managed to find Inspector Blake, and conductor Jack. He managed to find both Bob Grant and Stephen Lewis at the same time, whilst producing a television show called *Mrs Wilson's Diaries*, in which both Bob and Stephen appeared in the same episode. Impressed with what he saw in them, Allen suggested they be the conductor and the inspector. Bob and Stephen, who had worked together in the past at Joan Littlewood's Theatre workshop in Stratford East, had an excellent onscreen chemistry, and had in the past written and acted together on many occasions.

The next step in casting was to put a face to the miserable Arthur, Olive's husband and Stan's brother-in-law. "That one was easy," said Ronnie Wolfe. "We were thinking about who we could get to be Arthur, and by an amazing bit of luck we spotted Michael Robbins on television that very evening. He was on *The Harry Worth Show* and what character was he playing? A passenger on the bus! That was all we needed to see, and we had found the fourth member of our team."

But Michael only just made the bus. He could have easily been a dustman.

"Mike had a very lean patch of work," his widow, actress Hal Dyer explained. "The very week that *On the Buses* was offered to him, he had another offer in the post, for the Granada series *The Dustbinmen*. I've no idea what character he would be playing, but he nearly got the part. He knew Trevor Bannister, and they even sent him a script. He debated it for a while, but thankfully he chose *On the Buses*."

Remaining to be cast were the two ladies of Luxton: the Butler's mother, Mabel Ethel Butler, and Olive Rudge, Stan's sister.

"We had interviews for all the cast," director Howard Ross

explained. "All apart from Mum. Stuart Allen had the idea to have Cicely Courtneidge. He'd either worked with her before, or her husband, but he wanted her on board."

For the first series, the renowned stage actress Dame Cicely Courtneidge was the matriarch of the Butler household. "That was certainly one of Stuart Allen's choices," Ronald Chesney confirmed. "It was quite a radical idea, as Cicely was very much a stage actress and she was a very popular lady. It was no doubt that she would be a great boost to the show and help get it on the road to popularity. Amazingly, she agreed to the part and we were quite delighted."

But Cicely couldn't stay forever, and with a pre-arranged commitment in a theatre production waiting for her in the West End, the second series had to make do with a different mother.

"I love her dearly, but she wasn't a team player," Howard Ross recalled. "She was a huge star, but it was clear in the early days it wouldn't work too well with her."

With Doris Hare returning from Mexico at just the right time, it looked like divine intervention had another chance to work its magic. "Doris was fantastic in the part," recalled Ronald Chesney. "It had been arranged before, that if she could do it, she would, but when the first series aired her husband, Dr John Roberts, who was a professor of something, had been over in Mexico with her and she was unavailable. She had been on the stage since she was a baby, and her experience was astonishing. Reg was keen to have her in the show too. Cicely was good, but she had trouble with her lines. She said that if we ever went on tour, she would learn the script like a play, but with television, she found it difficult. There was no doubting Doris was the perfect cockney mum for us, and we had chosen right in Doris."

The final cog in the machinery was Olive, the lardy, four-eyed frump, who, clad more often than not in plain brown dresses and boring hairstyles, brought an incredible facade of drabness to Luxton. Behind the glasses and shoulder-length brown wig lay Anna Karen, a pretty actress who was more than happy to 'de-glam' for Olive. "We found Anna by accident," Ronald Chesney explained. "She had a small part in a show we had written for the BBC, called *Wild, Wild, Women*. She turned up to rehearsals one day, I think she had flu, and she didn't look her best. I turned to Ronnie and said, 'She could be Olive!' We asked her if she wanted to come over to meet our producer for the part, and she agreed."

But Anna's actions on the way to the studio could have cost her the part. "I was driving," Chesney continued. "And I saw in the mirror, she was putting on lipstick and making up, so I had to turn back and say, 'No stop, you're supposed to look terrible!' But on arrival to the studios she looked perfect, just as we had hoped."

Anna Karen remembers her casting in *On the Buses* well. "I did *Carry On Camping* with Barbara Windsor first, and I was booked because they needed a tall girl," Karen explained. "She told me about a part going in *Wild Wild Women*, I went along to the show to see what parts were going, and met the writers. They told me about *On the Buses* and asked me to go over to LWT with them, and I got in the car and went to the studios. On the way, I decided to put on some make-up, and Ronnie Chesney turned round and said, 'No, no, no! We need to you to look like you do now!'. It's just as well really, as I probably wouldn't have got the part otherwise!"

With all the cast in place, the show was coming together, and with an impressive line-up of talent, the possibilities of success were greatly enhanced. "The casting was the key to the show," Anna Karen explained. "It was very well cast. I wasn't experienced enough at the time to think about the potential of the show, or whether it would work. It was January, work was slim, and it was just a job, so that was it, but it worked out so well. I was delighted to be in the show, it was all quite new for me. Bob and Stephen were old friends, but most of us didn't know each other. It took a little while to get to know each other, but we all got on well in the end. Especially me and

Michael, he was always a good laugh!"

Writing the First Episode

They had the cast, a producer, and the green light to proceed. The most crucial ingredient to the sitcom remained; put together a script that will demonstrate the humour. "We had

Coming to bed now Arthur?

One of the eternal questions about *On the Buses*, is how fate ever drew together Olive and Arthur into marriage. The reason is hinted in the Series Six episode 'Stan's Worst Day', in which Stan recalls how Arthur moved into the house, accidentally and harmlessly ended up in Olive's bed, and was forced to marry her by mum. Anna Karen thinks some illegitimacy was behind the fateful attraction. "I think in one episode it's hinted that Olive is pregnant," she explained. "There was a hint there, and I think that's how they got together. That's my theory anyway!"

presented a pilot idea to Frank Muir," Wolfe remembers. "It was a good six pages in length. We also gave a rough synopsis of the other five episodes, we were keen to illustrate the potential to him.

"We often started writing an episode with just one word on the page. One of the favourite *On the Buses* episodes is called 'The New Uniforms' and we that was built up and revolved just around one word 'uniform'. We both sat down and thought what the angle could be, what the possibilities were, why would Blakey change the uniforms - are the busmen doing dirty DIY jobs in them? It seemed visually good, so we decided on that."

Wolfe and Chesney also took inspiration from newspapers and press to summon ideas for episodes. "We read in the paper at the time, that bus conductors lived longer than bus drivers" recalled Ronald Chesney. "The conductor lived about five years longer. He was running up and down the stairs all day, keeping fit, whereas the driver was in the cab sitting down all day." This article transformed itself onto the screen, in the form of Series Four episode 'Dangerous Driving' (also referred to as 'Dangerous Living').

Developing the Characters

The characters in *On the Buses* became household names. Blakey's trademark laugh, Jack's wide smirk, and Olive's thick glasses all helped towards making a set of unique, original, and funny characters.

To get in the mood of the characters they were playing,

The Singing Bus Driver

It has been rumoured that the development of Stan Butler was partly based on crooner Matt Monro, a man commonly referred to as the singing bus driver. Being of a similar height and stature, Monro could have been the perfect model for Reg Varney to build his character, and the pair were in fact friends. "Matt and Reg knew each other fairly well," explained Matt Monro's daughter Michele. "They would all see each other on the circuit. I don't recall anyone pointing [the similarities between them] out, but it is possible it was mentioned. I know for a fact it was said Matt looked like Patrick Wymark, but not Reg. Dad did, however, appear on Reg Varney's show *The Reg Varney Revue* in 1972 singing *Chattanooga Choo Choo* and *Curiouser and Curiouser*, but I'm afraid I don't know of any other connection."

Writers Ronald Wolfe and Ronald Chesney are aware of the similarities, but stress there is no deliberate connection; "I think it was just a coincidence."

some cast members took it upon themselves to do some advance research. "Reg and Stephen both went to Wood Green bus depot" Anna Karen explained. "This was all before the series started, they went on a visit there to see what it was like working on the buses."

As far as altering their appearance to get into the persona of the newly dreamt up characters, the majority of the cast needed little adjustment for the part. Reg Varney, Bob Grant, Cicely Courtneidge and later Doris Hare only required a change of clothes and standard make-up and hairstyling, but other characters were more challenging. To become Blakey, Stephen Lewis had to have the addition of a small toothbrush moustache, and to disguise the fact that in reality he was twenty years younger than Reg Varney, his appearance had to be aged with clever use of make-up. Equally to make Reg Varney look less like his actual 53-year-old self, and more like the 40-something he was meant to play, the use of make-up played an important part. Incredibly, despite the large age gap between Stephen and Reg, the effect was carried off supremely.

Perhaps the biggest appearance transformation came with Anna Karen, who played Olive. Only a few years before being cast in *On the Buses*, she was working as a dancer at the Panama Club, but now she had to become the beacon of blandness.

"Once I'd see the part, I was determined to make Olive the ugliest woman on television!"

"I remember the chat we had with the producer," Ronald Chesney explained. "He said to Anna; 'It's quite a nasty part, Anna, you have to look ugly, with thick glasses, and when you go to bed at night, you have to take you teeth out'. Anna promptly took out her back teeth, and she never put them back in for the episodes and films!"

Thankfully, Anna was happy to dull down, and actually enjoyed it. "I loved it," she laughed. "Once I'd seen the part I was determined to make Olive the ugliest woman on television. I loved to put on the padding and the glasses, it was wonderful doing it. I had the Olive wig made so it had a very flat top, it was very unflattering, with the centre parting. I had a lot of influence in Olive. Whenever I went out, I always got people saying, 'Oh you look a lot better than you do on telly', which was brilliant as opposed to the glamorous ladies who have to maintain that onscreen image when they go to the shops. One occasion, which did annoy me, though was on a train. I was tired, it had been a long day, and this woman really did wind me up. She pointed at me and said, 'Look at the state of her, you think she'd dress up to go out', I couldn't believe it!"

Another trait of Olive was her bottomless stomach, and food seldom seemed to be off her mind. "Olive ate a lot," Anna continued. "I had to eat quite often in scenes, usually I just pushed it about on the plate as it wasn't the nicest food. I think it came from the LWT canteen, but under studio lights it lost appeal. I did have to eat with my left hand though, as I was always on the end of the table with the cameras to my right, so I had to use the other hand so not to block my face when I ate."

Karen's work in moulding the character paid off. "The effect was wonderful. I did think I was going a bit too far until we went on production, and it was only then I saw it was a good result. The character itself I had based on someone I went to school with."

Olive, together with husband Arthur, became one of the most popular features of *On the Buses.* The frequent bickering between the duo rang many bells with unhappily married viewers, and the jibes and put-downs that would fly between them secured plentiful laughs. But Arthur's surly persona required some out-of-character acting from Michael Robbins. "He was always cast as the 'Cor Blimey' types," explained his widow, Hal. "It was either a 'hard man' or a 'bastard', but he certainly wasn't like that offscreen. He was quite a well-read, well-spoken man, and even trained to be a priest. Women used to come up and hit him with their handbag saying 'I'm married to a bugger like you', but that was part of the fun in his part. We always said it was disgusting the way he treated poor Olive - thankfully, he didn't take any inspiration from domestic life for that. Arthur was very much a chauvinist."

Designing for the Screen

Making the series come to life on the screen was the most important aspect of creating *On the Buses*, and Wolfe and Chesney had a lot of input into the end results. "It was so important for the bus depot to look realistic," Ronald Wolfe explained. "It had to look like a real depot. We always wanted to use real buses, and LWT were very good in letting us do it."

Getting them buses out...

When it came to finding buses to borrow, the production team found very few operators were enthusiastic to help.

"We just had to have real buses," explained Ronald Wolfe. "Having real buses just added to the show and made it more realistic. *On the Buses* could not have happened without buses."

But London's largest and most respected bus operator, London Transport, wanted no part of the charade. "The director wrote a letter to them and asked to use LT buses," Wolfe continued. "They just came back with a letter saying 'No'. They thought the idea of us having lazy, work-skiving drivers would give them a bad reputation. That letter was framed and hung in the office for a while!"

Thankfully, another London bus operator was keener on the idea. Eastern National buses, who had a main depot in Wood Green, London, were happy to let LWT use their vehicles, and supplied all the vehicles seen in the television series.

"Eastern National were very helpful to us, and were co-operative beyond the call of duty," explained director Howard Ross. "We wanted to get away from the red London Transport buses anyway really. Eastern National were based in Wood Green, so we used their bus depot for filming too."

However, in using the depot, the production team had to make some subtle changes to its exterior. "We had this big hoarding up outside Wood Green depot proclaiming it to be the Luxton Bus Company," Ronald Chesney recalled. "The public thought that Eastern National had changed its name. Of course, we also had the bus route for the show, which was the number 11 to the Cemetery Gates. We also found people were trying to get on our buses, even though they had no idea where the Cemetery Gates were."

It became apparent to the production team that if you put a bus stop somewhere, people would queue at it. "We often filmed in quiet streets where buses don't usually run," Chesney continued, "but as soon as we put a dummy bus stop there, we'd get a queue of passengers waiting for it!"

Eastern National was also very kind in allowing members of the cast to gain experience of what being on the buses actually entailed. Reg Varney paid several visits to the bus company's Basildon depot to improve his knowledge of working on the buses and also take his driving test - Reg was legally licensed to drive the bus, so long as he didn't carry passengers.

Eastern National drivers were only too keen to help the pro-gramme, especially as the one who drove a bus to the studios in Wembley would be entitled to some extra overtime. The buses would be delivered usually on a Saturday, stay at the studios all day Sunday for the recording, and then be brought back on Monday. Another popular exploit of the drivers was to try and take a recently returned bus out on service without changing the destination blinds. "We always had them returned with the Luxton and District sign on the side," recalls an anonymous retired EN driver. "That, and the Cemetery Gates blinds on the windows. There were a few occasions when the drivers would try and take the bus out with the fake Cemetery Gates blind on the bus. The inspector always managed to foil the plans, but I recall one occasion when the Luxton and District transfer stickers stayed on the side of a bus when it was taken out on service."

Sets

Originally the first series focused purely on the bus depot, the canteen, and the Butlers' house but as the show progressed, further sets were required including the manager's office, the depot lavatory, nurse's office, Jack's house, a chemist, a restaurant, and in the seventh series, even a Victorian street scene. All these sets had to be planned, designed and built in a matter of weeks.

Production designer David Catley was the first designer with *On the Buses* and worked on the first three episodes in 1969. For the remainder of the first series and the subsequent three series, Andrew Gardner, who after *On the Buses* went on to work with Wolfe and Chesney on *Romany Jones, Yus My Dear* and *Don't Drink the Water,* designed the sets throughout 1970. He handed over to Alan Hunter-Craig and Rodney Cammish for the remaining four series.

Alan Hunter-Craig was responsible for production design on the majority of *On the Buses* episodes, and was at the drawing board for forty-three programmes. He has fond memories of the show. "I was working freelance for many of the major TV stations," Alan explained. "I did find *On the Buses* quite funny and it was a nice, gentle show to work on. I got started in production design with the BBC. I was with them for six years as a trainee, out of five thousand applicants only twenty-four were chosen. We were all from different backgrounds graphics, architects, sculptors, and they all thought they could train us and use us. I became an assistant production designer, then a designer, and then I left the BBC to work freelance."

As a freelance designer, Hunter-Craig joined *On the Buses* initially as production designer and progressed to production design supervisor, in charge of the design team who built and dressed the sets. "We had a large team," he recalls, "-made up of painters, dressers, buyers and contractors who were brought in from outside. It was a big team."

Alan joined the *On the Buses* team in the forth series, so previous designers had already come up with the major sets for the programme. "The standing sets [the Butlers' house and the depot] were already done, but there was always the need for additional sets if we did a pub scene or the manager's office. I redesigned the canteen myself and had a big girder put in the middle. I thought that it suited the canteen better."

The main problem for the design team was making the sets stable. "In feature films, we had solid walls, nailed everything down into the ground, and even built solid plaster ceilings. But in television, everything had to be put up and down quickly, so we had to brace the sets from behind. It was very difficult to get the stability of the sets. Because we had the audience in as well. We had to have the sets open at open at one end so that they could see what was going on. We had the sets weighted, and propped, but there was often a wobble. Everything was very high pressure, but there were a lot of good times (and a lot of drinking to take our minds off it)."

"The design team were very good," recalls director Howard Ross. "With the sets, it would be both in house and exterior contractors who made them. It would be leased out to somewhere to make the basic sets, and then the LWT designers would tweak it about. We had them made from plywood rather than from canvas, like in theatres. Occasionally there would be a wobble, if someone knocked a door too hard it would wobble. If it was minor, we wouldn't retake it but a lot of the time it wasn't even noticed. When you have a tight schedule you have to be conscious of time and decide whether retakes are feasible."

Another problem about having the sets opened only at one end was the positioning of the dining table in the kitchen scenes. "We all had to shuffle round the sides of this table," Anna Karen recalls. "Nobody could have their back to the camera, so Reg was at the top of the table, Michael was on the side, and me and Doris were squeezed on the left. I do, however, remember the sets wobbled an awful lot."

Derrick Goodwin, who was the director of eighteen *On the Buses* episodes, also recalls how troublesome the sets could be. "The walls were forever wobbling," he explained. "The sets all changed over the series as new designers came and went, but there was always a problem with those walls, they were so difficult to support. They looked solid, but if anyone should lean on them, it would wobble, and that was clearly visible on camera. It is really embarrassing looking back on that now, because it is so painful to see, especially for a director. We had them braced and weighted from behind, but nothing seemed to work."

The Depot

"I remember doing some filming at Wood Green, we had a great big Luxton sign hanging outside the depot," explained designer Alan Hunter-Craig. "That was done prior to me joining the show, by a previous designer, but I do remember having to make the bus stops and shelters. I have been told that when we had the fake bus stops out on the road, people actually started queuing at them, it seems quite strange considering how the film crew would all have been there. I do also recall also going up to Chelmsford bus depot where Eastern National had another base. I'm not sure if we actually filmed there, or just got the buses from there."

The curse of Blakey

There is no doubt that Stephen Lewis, a multi-talented writer, actor and performer, made his character in *On the Buses* his own. In fact, he developed the martinet Blakey so well that his character became the one most associated with the programme, something that made his iconic role a rather bitter subject within the rest of the cast, especially the better known performers, Reg Varney and Doris Hare.

"Reg was jealous of Stephen for a time," explained Anna Karen. "Reg always got the billing on the programmes but Stephen managed to steal the shows and really made the programme his own. Reg, of course, was a comic, a very good strong comic and he felt a little threatened by this. All comics can be insecure. But Stephen became the star, his mannerisms as Blakey and his acting made him really popular. He'd get a line saying 'Oh no', and he'd manage to stretch it out and exaggerate it for ages."

As well as ruffling the feathers of leading man Reg Varney, a slight clash in personality also put Blakey up against the matriarch of the Butler household, Doris Hare.

"Stephen was always a bit of an enigma," recalled Michael Robbins's widow, Hal Dyer. "He kept himself to himself, he was always quite distant when not filming the show. He didn't get on with Doris at all offscreen, he was quite Left-wing, and she was a very grand lady, so there was a clash there. He often tried to send her up, and there are a few scenes at the dinner tables where there were crossed knives."

Stephen's clash with Doris also came to the attention of actress Ursula Mohan. "Stephen always thought someone like Doris didn't think much of him. Doris was an incredible performer. Her CV was as long as her body but I remember once he said to us all 'Ooh, she 'ates us'. Now, I'm a visiting actress so I never liked to get involved with politics on a show where a group of people have to work with each other every week but that was something that surprised me."

Unfortunately, Stephen Lewis's accomplished individual work as Blakey also led to strained relations with other production members. "He was very good in the part," explained Ronald Chesney. "But outside the show he was a bit mad really!" Another source close to *On the Buses*, suggesting Lewis was difficult to work with, remarked, rather unfairly, "The show was great...if it wasn't for Stephen."

Having built his character up to such a strong reputation in *On the Buses*, Lewis struggled with being type-cast after he left the programme. Having reprised his role of Blakey in *Don't Drink the Water,* and a very Blakey-like stint in *Oh Doctor Beeching* and latterly *Last of the Summer Wine*, Stephen disappeared from the lime-light in 2006.

Like Bob Grant, who vanished from his friends and colleagues for more than eleven years until his death, Stephen Lewis has taken to a reclusive life and has left many of his friends and colleagues guessing where he is. "I have no idea where he is at the minute," Anna Karen continued. "My friend Kate Williams doesn't know, none of the people I contact know either - he has really hidden himself away, which is a shame. The last I'd heard he had gone to live with his sister."

Perhaps the closest link in the acting world to Lewis, actor Brian Murphy, has also been left wondering. "I've known Stephen for a very long time." Brian explained. "I even watched his audition at Joan Littlewood's for the very first time, and I've worked with him in the past, most notably in *Last of the Summer Wine*. But I haven't seen him for a good few years. We had a dinner event for the cast of *Summer Wine*, which he came along to. I asked how he was keeping and he said; 'I'm all right' and that was about it. I haven't seen him since."

Lewis, who until recently lived in Greenwich, was last in the newspapers in 2008, when *The Sun* ran a small feature on him crashing his red Ford Fiesta into a bus stop in Lee, Southeast London.

Since retiring as an actor, Lewis has cut ties with his previous agents, who hold no details on his location. Even the brand licensing department at ITV, who presumably continue to pay royalties to Lewis for his television work, claim to have no current details for him.

The actual Eastern National bus depot only featured fleetingly, with just a few seconds of location footage used in the episodes, to give the viewer a sense of the bus arriving at the depot. The majority of depot scenes were recreated at Wembley Studios. "We knew the size of the bus, and the position it needed to be in, so the bus station scenes were fairly easy to do," explained Hunter-Craig. "With such a big bus, if the camera went too far back to try and get the bus roof in shot, it would show the top of the studio as well. So we had what we called 'degree angles'. These were the angles that the camera needed to shoot from, and we usually discussed these with the director."

The buses put further problems in the way. Throughout the course of *On the Buses*, the addition of wooden boards are visible under the bus wheels in the studio, and these were allegedly added to prevent the bus making indentations to the studio floor. "I don't personally remember this," Alan explained. "With television studios, it would be a thick concrete floor topped with a layer of lino, so the floor would be very solid, but the lino on top could have been getting warped."

Real buses did, however, promote additional hurdles for the production team. In a small studio, with more than two hundred audience members present, the fumes the engines emitted could have presented quite serious air quality problems. When it was decided to run the monstrous six-cylinder Gardner bus engine, exhaust fumes could have been lethal.

To prevent this deadly formula, a special tube was added to the exhaust pipe, to extend it outside of the studio block, and transfer the fumes out of the studio.

"We seldom ran the bus engines in the studio," explained sound supervisor Paul Faraday. "Aside from the sound problems it would cause for my team, it was just too awkward. On the rare occasion we did, the fumes would have to be diverted, otherwise the audience would have been killed."

Props

Once the sets were in place, they would need to be dressed with furniture and props. "All the furniture would have been hired from many different companies," recalled designer Alan Hunter-Craig. "I went along to these places with the buyer, and decided what to get for the show. We usually had a props list from the director, and we picked all the stuff we needed. Pictures for the wall, cutlery for the dinner tables, and bits of tat for the sideboard. The only thing we wouldn't get were action props [such as photographs mocked up especially for the episode] - these would have been down to the producer to arrange."

Occasionally, the prop hire company would be given back less than was hired from them. "Things went missing all the time," Alan continued. "If someone took a shine to a particular photograph or figurine, it would be taken. Things had a habit of walking."

Ronald Wolfe recalls how often the props went adrift. "The staff, the floor managers, and the cast took everything," he explained. "Whatever was in the fridge at the end of the show was taken, they all made sure they got their bit."

The pictures on the walls were guarded carefully. If these went adrift, LWT would need to foot some hefty bills. Incredibly, some of these discrete paintings hanging on the walls of the Butlers' living room could well have been rare, original productions worth hundreds of pounds. "A lot of the paintings were genuine oils," Alan Hunter-Craig explained. "The prop hire companies lent these out because they could charge a percentage of the value to the TV company. With fake pictures, they couldn't do this, so there was a fair chance that On the Buses had a few rarities on the wall."

In Series Seven, when the *On the Buses* was recorded at South Bank Studios, a prop bus had to be created. The doors to the studio were too low for a double decker to be brought in, so single deckers were used with wooden mock-up roofs lowered onto them from the studio's lighting rig.

Designer Alan Hunter-Craig remembered, "We sometimes had the fake bus fronts in the later series, but it was usually a real one all the action was done around. The production team could easily have put together a mock-up for use on the show; they were very creative. I later worked again with Derrick Goodwin on *The Train Now Standing* and that required us to build a train station in the studio."

But any fake buses that were created would not have been around long. "At the end of the series, they would have all been smashed up and chucked out." Alan continued. "It was a shocking waste, and the cost of building them and then throwing them out was quite enormous."

For close-ups, a mock-up was created by studio carpenters, made up with parts from Eastern National's bus bodybuilders in Lowestoft, and boasting a fleet number plate (2552 - which still exists) and registration number YDU 265D. These mock-ups had no back end, so logistically filming was made a great deal easier, and they also used older seat patterns than the real ones, so they can always be told apart from the genuine buses.

Uniform

Designed and styled in-house by costumers at LWT, the Luxton and District busmen's uniform really brought the characters to life and managed to promote several additional scenarios for comedy in the series, namely Stan's abuse of the company's clothing. In charge of the tailor's chalk and designer of the uniform was costume designer Vee Layton.

Vee, who was married to the prominent actor and guest *On the Buses* co-writer George Layton, worked her magic on many of LWT's flagships programmes of the era. "She was an eminent and talented designer," George Layton fondly recalls. "Working on ground-breaking shows in the 70s like *Budgie, Doctor in the House, Upstairs Downstairs* and, of course, *On the Buses*. Sadly, Vee died in 2010."

Ursula Mohan, one of the show's most frequent supporting artists, remembered the dressing process. "If I recall, we went for a fitting first, and they designed the costume and made it around us. The designers were very good, I remember at one point I even wore my own dress for an episode, it was this grey snake skin skirt and it was for the location part on 'Private Hire'. I saw that episode again recently and I was astonished to see my skirt again, I loved that dress, sadly I don't have it any more!"

"The uniforms we had made were fairly standard," director Howard Ross recalls. "I think it was just the basic bus driver and conductor uniform, and we added the Luxton badges and things on to them. Once we broadcast, the costumes would have stayed with us for a while, and then probably been sold on to a costumers somewhere. LWT didn't have the wardrobe space of the BBC, and when we moved studios as well we had even less space!"

· 4 ·

Behind the Scenes

<u>London Weekend Television</u>

LWT started life as a creation of the London Television Consortium, who had drawn up a plan for a new London weekend broadcaster to take over from ATV London in a reallocation of franchises. The plan promised strong programming with a variation of high-end drama and cultural broadcasting an idea, which the Independent Television Authority approved believing that the formula could rival the BBC.

In 1968, the London weekend franchise was awarded to the consortium who went on to christen the newly formed, and aptly named, programme producer London Weekend Television. Making good on their promise of high-brow arts, LWT produced mainly Shakespearean plays, and recorded concerts including *Barbara Dickson at the Albert Hall* and *King of Violinists.*

Understandably, with programming failing to meet the spectrum of entertainment viewers were anticipating, audiences soon deserted the newly formed channel in favour of BBC's mass-appeal weekend entertainment. LWT struggled through its first year, with dismal ratings. Strike action added further to the misery, and the first technicians' walk-out occurred less than one minute into LWT's first programme, on 2nd August 1968, a result of a dispute sparked by technicians wanting additional pay to work the weekend shifts.

The problems continued. With low viewing figures and an ever present fear of a strike, LWT was forced to the brink of collapse. However, intervention by the Australian media mogul Rupert Murdoch, who purchased a large stake in the company in 1969, put the station back on the road. Yet Murdoch was not popular with many LWT executives, having already dispensed with the services of several board members within his first few weeks at the station. Despite promoting a gradual increase in business of LWT, Murdoch was forced out of a governing position by the IBA in 1971, to allow regular running of the station to resume.

With a change of studios in 1972, and mass-market programming, LWT gradually continued its expansion and lost the stigma connected to its first years in operation. The station continued to be successful throughout the early 1980s, despite some loss of jobs caused by industrial action and surviving the cruel Ken Dodd remark that the station name stood for "long wait for a titter." LWT remained as weekend broadcaster for London until 1990, when the new broadcasting act was introduced, which forced a change in how contracts were awarded to different television stations.

With competitive rival contract bidding ensuing, and the London weekday franchisee, Thames, losing its contract to Carlton in 1992, LWT itself was eventually taken over by Granada in 1994. Granada continued a hostile battle to win all the other regional broadcasters, and by 2001, they were in a position to own the entire English and Welsh television network, deciding to rebrand the network as ITV1. The LWT name lingered on the credis of most London productions until 31st October 2004, when the generic ITV Studios trademark became the standard production company name on all national and

Behind the Scenes

regional ITV programmes. What started off as a small station with poor fortunes had lasted an astonishing thirty-six years.

How to talk like the a Luxton resident

Pronunciation of certain words are noticeably different in Luxton and its surrounding districts. This handy little guide will assist you in conversing with local residents.

- "os" as in 'ostrich' is pronounced "ors" as in 'horse'.
example: "I'm taking Olive to the 'orspital.

- "As" as in 'asterix' is pronounced "Ars" as in 'cars'
example: "Mum makes a smashing Cornish parsty"

- "on" as in 'on' is pronounced "awn" as in 'warning'.
example: "he's gawn out"

- "Hs" are dropped on many words.
example: "I 'ate you Butler"

- "Gs" are often dropped off the end of words.
example: "Get the chips Jack, I'm starvin'"

- "Thur" as in 'Thursday' is pronounced as "fer" as in 'refer'.
example: "Arfer, your dinner's ready!"

Once you have completed this exercise in pronunciation, remember to repeat the following phrase to correct your diction back to normal standards: "Hunting hounds have hardly ever harkened to handsome Harold's hunting horn."

Changing Studios

On the Buses was filmed at two different television studios over its lengthy five-year run on LWT. For the first six series, Wembley Studios, the largest London production base was utilised, with all production moving to the newly opened South Bank studios for the seventh and final series, in 1972.

Wembley Park Studios opened in 1926, originally as a base for British Talking Pictures. By the early 1930s, ownership had fallen to Fox Films, and later Rayment Films, before Associated Rediffusion expanded the site and made Wembley their main television base in 1960.

When the London weekend franchise was awarded to London Weekend Television in 1968, Wembley studios became the station's main production base, and the majority of their programmes including On the Buses, were filmed there, often with exterior location footage being recorded in the local area.

Despite having enviable production facilities, including a large soundproofed curtain that could be lowered to turn the main studio into two individual production rooms, LWT were keen to expand their technology, and chose to develop a new studio, on the south side of the River Thames.

Building for the new South Bank Studios commenced in 1970, and the gradual move of production was begun in 1972, with the nine studio rooms inside the complex becoming fully operational in 1974.

Rehearsals

An episode of *On the Buses* had a turnaround faster than the Number 11 itself. Within a matter of days an episode could be written, rehearsed and recorded ready for transmission.

"It was all done very quickly," recalled Anna Karen. "We did an episode a week usually. We'd go to rehearsals on at the start of the week, which were always in Wembley, and then recorded it at the end of the week, then we'd be back rehearsing next week's one the next day."

The speed of getting a show together took its toll on everyone, especially the production team who were incredibly conscious of getting finished the tasks on time. "The turnaround was a very exhausting one," director Howard Ross explains. "We had scripts arriving sometimes only in the first rehearsals, the writers were being pushed to churn them out on a weekly basis. On the first series all the scripts were in the office weeks before, but that wasn't a case with the later ones. I remember one instance we all sat down for the read-through, and I was literally handed the script there and then, we were all literally reading it for the first time there and then as we went along!"

Rehearsals for *On the Buses* were usually always held in the same place, the LWT tower block, Station House, which was located at Stonebridge Park in north London. "It was an office block, but we had two floors of rehearsal rooms," Howard Ross continued. "We were on the twelfth floor, with light entertainment and variety. It was an exciting floor, and in general just an exciting time, I think the rest of the company were jealous of our floor!"

As taxing as working on a major television show with tight deadlines were, there was always fun to be had whilst the cast waited for their scenes to come up during rehearsals. "We had these paper aeroplane contests during rehearsals," Anna Karen laughed. "We were on the top floor, and we made planes out of script pages and threw them out of the window; it was usually Stephen who won them. Me and Michael had some great laughs too. The costume people had these clothing rails on wheels, so we used to stand on them and race down the corridors. We made up songs together too, and he'd change the words to songs and made me laugh, he was such fun to work with."

In the Studio

On the Buses usually consisted of a fairly large studio team; with four camera operators, a floor sound crew, a director, producer, designer, writers, and vision mixer in the gallery, plus several runners and floor managers.

The production staff of the show was rotational, and each camera and sound crew took turns in working behind the scenes of *On the Buses.* "Nobody did a full run of a series, it was rotational," confirmed Paul Faraday, an ex-LWT sound supervisor. "Each team would have done some programmes of each series, but it would never have been the same crew responsible for a full series."

Using real buses could sometimes be problematic for the sound crew, and especially the use of double-deckers. "Occasionally, the director wanted a long shot across the studio to show the audience the full size of the bus," continued Paul. "He then wanted us to record a conversation between the cast next to the bus, and it was difficult getting the boom microphones and fish-poles to the cast without them being seen on the camera. We never used radio microphones; they were just too unreliable. Of course, when we moved to South Bank studios, this problem was solved, as the doubledecker's couldn't get in the studio doors, so we had to use fake, buses - much quieter."

The noise of the bus in the studio could also be troublesome, so running the engine was avoided wherever possible. "Almost all the time, the engine noises heard would be sound effects. We had a huge library of effects, so we could supply whatever the director wanted. I don't think we ever ran the bus engines in the studio, the main reason being that we'd have to pipe out all the fumes or the audience would be killed."

Bus engine noises were not necessarily one of the sounds that pre-existed in the LWT library, so these had to be captured especially for the show, and were recorded at Wood Green bus depot. "I visited Wood Green in 1968/9 and a Luxton and District Lodekka was being used for sound recording," a former conductor at EN reminisced. "It was being driven round with the bottom of the stairs lifted and a microphone held by the gearbox. So although the main buses used in the show were 2930 and 2917, the sounds you heard were likely from a totally different bus."

An aspect, which didn't need any sound effects, was the laughter of the audience. "We never dubbed was the laughter track," Paul Faraday explained. "With *On the Buses*, the audience fell about laughing all the time, so we just didn't have to. We used microphones from the studio ceiling to capture their reactions, and that went straight onto the episode. Only once or twice, for continuity, the laughter track would be placed over two joining clips if there were problems with the sound."

Keeping the laughter authentic was also something that the show's creators were very keen on. "We never wanted to dub laughter onto the show," explained Ronald Chesney. "We had an audience, and if they didn't laugh, it wasn't a funny show. We didn't want to put on laughter where it shouldn't have been."

But occasionally, having the audience's reactions recorded onto the programme could be construed as a mistake, as in one episode of *On the Buses*, 'The Squeeze', several remarks made by the audience can be heard. In one such instance, a woman's voice saying, "Look at his face in there!" can be heard when Blakey is shown stuck in the motorcycle sidecar. During the episode 'Stan's Worst Day', another audience member can be heard, this time remaking, "He's gone in the wrong bed!" when Arthur pads around the house. Equally, in 'The Canteen Girl', a distinct "Oo-er!" can be heard when Molly attempts to enter Stan's room when he is trouserless.

Aside from the sound team, the other, and most important, half of the production crew was the team behind the visuals. Like the sound crews, the camera team and vision mixers were in close contact with the gallery to make sure they were getting the desired shots. "After we'd rehearsed, we'd put together a camera script," director Howard Ross explained. "The camera team would get one of these, and it would tell them who needed to film what and where. The vision mixer would also get one to follow, and from the gallery they would cut to each camera in turn. We had constant talkback from the box to the studio floor, so we could contact floor managers, add cutting points and take shots away. We had a very close relationship with the vision mixers, but once the show was finished they didn't do any further work with editing. Likewise with floor managers, you rarely saw them, they'd appear at rehearsal and then for the recording."

Warming Up

Getting the viewers in a jovial mood was the job of the *On the Buses* warm-up man. This coveted task was fulfilled by many over the years. In the very early days it was co-writer Ronald Chesney but as the show progressed, the comedian Felix Bowness took over the part.

"It was usually Felix Bowness who did the audience warm-ups," confirmed Ronald Wolfe. "He was very good and he got the audience laughing, which is just what we wanted. I think Michael Grade did some audience warm-ups too." However Michael Grade, later controller of BBC1 and now, like his uncles, a member of the House of Lords, denies his involvement, explaining "*On the Buses* had just finished before I arrived at London Weekend Television, sorry."

Another warm-up man was also a familiar face on the screen. "My husband, Terry Duggan, did some of the shows too," explained Anna Karen. "He had done a few warm-ups on the show in the past, but when Derek Goodwin became the director he took on the role full-time. Brian Izzard did the final series, and brought his own warm-up man, but the majority of the time it was Felix, Terry or Michael."

The Production Process

The casual viewer seldom thinks in depth about the work that goes in to producing a television programme. Yet for *On the Buses*, planning an episode of just twenty-five minutes in length was a process that started months before.

"The first step was the scripts," Ronald Chesney explained. "We did a few rough notes of script ideas before each series, and then started writing the scripts."

All the scripts for *On the Buses* were written by hand, with Ronald Wolfe's wife, Rose, painstakingly typing them up afterwards. "I used a manual typewriter - not even an electric one," Rose explained. "I typed every episode, even the films. The two Ronnies were very good with sharing the writing of each script. One week, Wolfe would go to Chesney's house in Kingston, and the next Chesney would come up to ours in Golders Green."

Once the first script was finished, the cast would be issued with a copy to learn lines and movements, and the producer, director and designer would also be handed a copy.

"I got the scripts about three weeks before the recording," explained designer Alan Hunter-Craig. "I'd read through it, and work out what sets, scenery and props were needed. If we needed elevations, like stairs, then we would have contractors brought in to do that, so that took time to plan too. Then we had to talk all this over with the producer, and work out the cost and the budget. We then talked over all this with the camera operators, lighting, sound crew and floor managers."

"We met with the designers, producers and camera crew a week before recording," confirmed sound supervisor Paul Faraday. "Rehearsals would be done at Station House in Wembley, we'd attended the day before to see what the scripts were like and where everyone would be, and then we could think about where the microphones should be placed to best pick up the sound."

"I remember the crew would all meet and discuss the episode before we went to the first rehearsal," concurred director Derrick Goodwin. "The budget was usually the first thing on the agenda, for me at least. We usually did an episode of *On the Buses* for about £9,000. My salary was fairly basic, and I certainly never saw any repeat fees, but some of the cast were on quite basic pay too, it was usually between £40 and £70 per episode."

Once the first production meeting for the series had been completed, the cast of the show would congregate to read through the scripts. "LWT had a tower block on the North Circular Road in London," explained Stuart Allen in a 1971 interview. "We all gathered there for the read-through on the first day of the week. This involves reading the script once through, and drinking about twenty cups of coffee each. The net result

Arthur and Olive's future together

It doesn't take a genius to notice how Olive and Arthur's relationship can appear, at times, strained. After ten years together, the two once flourishing lovebirds could do with some assistance.

In attempt to rejuvenate the passion in their partnership, professional marriage guidance councillor Dominic Keeran (MSW), who holds an MA degree from the Kent School of Social Work, and with more than thirty years' experience in the field of private practice, has genuinely been consulted for his opinion.

Olive (Luxton) asks...
"I didn't know my husband very long before we married.

We were both coaxed into matrimony by my widowed mother who discovered us in bed together. I was thrilled when we did marry, and thought we had a future together, and I think Arthur felt the same, but we've been together ten years now, and I think things are starting to lose their magic.

Things didn't start well after our honeymoon in Grimsby, my newlywed carried me over the threshold of the house back in Luxton, and he ruptured himself lifting me up and needed an operation. He hasn't been the same since. This, of course, means intimacy is difficult for him now, so enjoyment has faded from our relationship in that sense. But it's mainly the love that I think has gone. When my husband comes home, he'll just watch the football on telly and doesn't talk to me too often, Id cook him dinner and he'd insult it. I've seen him flirting with other women at the darts match, too. I'm no saint, I too have flirted, but only to see if I can make him jealous and realise what he has with me.

Things have never got violent with Arthur, but we have come close to blows many times, and he has threatened to belt me if I cheated - in a way I think this just proves that deep down he does love me.

I try and rekindle our relationship whenever possible, I suggest we have an early night, I'm just not sure what we can do. We have our moments, but I don't think we have much of a future left together. What do you think about our relationship?"

Dominic Keeran replies...

"The marriage relationship is something that requires much effort and attention. Things do not come naturally. Your husband may equate sex with love, so he thinks if he is excited less by you physically, then he does not love you and seeks excitement elsewhere. Spirituality can offer depth of meaning that marriage needs as time goes by. Let him know you feel sadness about changes in your relationship, that you miss him, and your desire to put effort into it. Good luck."

of a read through is a lot of coffee-sodden scripts. Then [the producer] plotted through the movements for the actors and take them through scene by scene."

After the first read-through at Station House, the cast and crew would meet for a second rehearsal later in the week, and a final dress rehearsal at Wembley Studios.

"As writers, we always attended the rehearsals," explained Ronald Wolfe. "It was important for us to make sure the cast were happy with the lines. We usually had a few scripts put by before the rehearsals of the first episode. We often wrote the next episode whilst they were rehearsing the first next door!"

The day of the recording was usually a Sunday. "We did the recordings in the evening, having already done a dress rehearsal in the morning," explained designer Alan Hunter-Craig. "The sets would have been brought in the night before and through the night, the painters and carpenters would be fixing it all up, and making good all the wallpaper on the walls, bringing in the furniture and arranging it for the shoot the next day."

Make-up and costume would be done shortly before recording. "We usually waited until recording before the cast went to make-up," director Howard Ross explained. "Sometimes, usually with the ladies, we had make-up done before the dress rehearsals. The men didn't need much makeup. Blakey was the only one really, as he had to have his moustache added on. There was an age difference between Stephen and Reg, but we didn't age him up too much, just a little shadowing on his face maybe. He did most of the work through facial expressions, he was a very good actor."

On the day of the recording, the audience were usually let in at 7pm, with the cameras rolling by half past seven. Should everything go to plan, the episode would be finished within an hour.

"We always had pauses in the episode recording," Ronald Chesney recalled. "Usually it was just to get the cast to change costumes, or to redo a take that didn't work as well. Sometimes we would use the gaps to go off and change the script if it didn't seem to work in certain parts."

With the episode in the can, the opening and closing titles would be added to the tape, and the episode would be prepared for broadcast, which was usually a month later.

"We didn't do much editing," director Howard Ross explained. "We tried to do the show all in one go, we used two-inch tape to film on, and this was charged to the episode - so as we cut to different cameras, it recorded and edited as we went along, so there was very little to do afterwards. That way we could make a programme without cutting the tape."

"The only time we did cut, was if there was a retake, but we didn't do many of them. If someone fluffed a line, it would often be overlooked, not because we were conscious of saving tape, but because the filming schedule was so very hectic and high-pressured."

In the meantime, the studio would be emptied and prepared for use by another production. "The scenery would be broken down and put back into storage," designer Alan Hunter-Craig recalled. "Any windows that were brought in for the set would be returned to where it was hired from. The stuff that wouldn't be used again would be smashed up and put in a skip. We managed to get the sets put up and brought down very quickly, usually after the show had been recorded the studio would emptied within a couple of hours."

Despite the hectic schedule, the majority of memories of working with On the Buses are positive. "Something that stands out for me, is just how happy a time it was," director Howard Ross reminisces. "We had moans and groans, there wasn't a great deal of socialising, but nobody was ever an outsider. It was a happy time."

Location Filming

Occasionally, location footage would be used in an episode. "We did most of the location stuff a good month in advance," explained director Derrick Goodwin. "This meant we had to watch our continuity and make sure everybody was wearing the same costumes, and had the same hairstyles. I don't know why we bothered with location stuff, because it is so embarrassing. The location footage was very grainy, poor quality, and it just stuck out like a sore thumb within a piece of studio footage, I cringe looking back at it."

Location filming, which was almost always undertaken in the local area to Wembley and South Bank studios, was played back to the audience during the episode recording so their reactions could be captured on audio. Occasionally, to save tape, footage is reused in different episodes. In 'The Cistern', a segment of film sees the bus being stopped by Blakey, and him looking down at the bus platform to see the Butler's toilet. This segment of film is used again in the subsequent episode, 'Radio Control'. Certain shots of Stan driving into the depot have also been frequently repeated, most notably in the episode 'The Inspector's Niece' Stan drives into the depot wearing a smart uniform and tie, yet a cut to the studio sees him in a scruffy jumper.

Finding places to film was the job of director Stuart Allen and assistant Howard Ross. "We didn't have such things as location managers then," Howard Ross explained. "So a lot of the time, we drove around Wembley and looked for places to film in. If we needed a house, we'd go and knock on some doors, cross their palm with silver!"

The majority of the time, people were more than happy to assist. "TV was a bit of a magic box back then," Howard Ross continued. "People were very keen to help us then, attitudes towards television have changed these days and it's very much taken for granted. Personally, I wouldn't want a film crew in the same street as me."

Behind the Scenes

At the time, location filming was usually undertaken with large television cameras, which meant logistically, it was exceptionally difficult to work with. "This was all a long time before mobile filming and VT filming," Howard continued. "To get sound we used boom microphones, but not studio booms, these were fish poles, we never had radio microphones. The main problem was traffic noise, it was a constant annoyance, but we just had to retake. We had more flexibility on location, it was still clock watching, but not as much as in the studio."

Footage captured by cameras on location wasn't the greatest quality, but one *On the Buses* director, Derrick Goodwin, was a pioneer to change this, and took inspiration from a football match. "A director friend of mine called Jim Goddard was talking about the camera we used for location filming," Goodwin recalled. "We both thought that the footage they produced was too poor to work with, so we thought about what we could do instead. We noticed how the BBC had small cameras behind the goals in football matches, to film any action from behind the net. They were very small, reliable cameras, so we asked about using them in a drama or situation comedy. We were eventually allowed too, and they were great, absolutely fantastic. When I went over to Canada to do some TV work, we used them most of the time, and back in Britain, they became the main choice to use in future. These days, the cameras are so small, it is quite amazing how fast everything has moved on, but the use of them has its origins with us!"

5

Lovely Pair of Bristols

The vehicles of choice for use in *On the Buses* were loaned from Eastern National Bus Company in London, who supplied the faithful green doubledeckers, the Bristol FLF/FLF6LX Lodekka.

Because all the buses used for filming were genuine vehicles, used on public routes and services when not at the studios, the exact bus used on the show varied frequently. There are several instances where the bus used for filming studio shots and location shots were totally different, for example the Series Two episode 'Bon Voyage', the bus on location at the Cemetery Gates bears a different fleet number and is adorned with different advertisement posters than the vehicle used in the studio shots a few moments later. Also in the episode 'The New Nurse' bus 2917 is used on location whereas the studio shots used 2930.

Most frequently used were buses 2917 (AEV 811F) and 2930 (AVW 399F), which appeared in the majority of episodes over the five-year run of the series. On occasion, 2885 (WNO973F), 2743 (EOO 585) and 2911 (WWC 741F) were also utilised, as were the drivers of them, who were paid overtime to deliver the vehicles to the studio.

In the final series of the show, when production moved studios to South Bank in London, it was discovered the height of the studio doors were too low to accommodate doubledecker vehicles. To get around this problem, four fake mock-up buses were introduced for filming, WG2551, WG2552, WG2560 and WG2652. Eastern National's body builders in Lowestoft supplied the parts for the creations, and even cast metal fleet plate numbers for them, with 2552 apparently still existing in a private collection. In the final series, the only real buses to appear in the studio were single decked Bristol MW vehicles.

As well as the standard Bristol Lodekka buses used in the programme, various other specialist vehicles were brought in. Most notably in the Series Six episode 'No Smoke without Fire' where a Leyland PD2 Routemaster OLD666 (RTL1557) is purposely set on fire and destroyed for the episode. In one of the final episodes, 'On the Omnibuses', a London General S454 bus appears, XL8 962. Perhaps the most specialist of all the vehicles ever used in the programme, the bus was built in 1922.

Coaches spring up a few times in the series too, such as the holiday coach in 'Family Flu' (a Bedford VAS MRO147D) and the pensioner's outing coach in 'Private hire' (a Bristol RESH/Duple Commander IV YTW538F - also borrowed from Eastern National, and one of only eleven ever built). When location filming switched from Wood Green depot to Nunhead Lane garage in Peckham, coaches appear regularly in the background - the depot was then occupied by Banfield's luxury coach company.

So what did the future hold for all the Luxton and District buses? The most prolific buses, fleet numbers 2917 and 2930 are still in existence. Bus 2917 is now residing in the United States, where it was exported in the 1990s by the Martin Luther King project, painted red, and transformed into a mobile library. In 1992, it was purchased by Buyabus where it lay awaiting an owner for five years before being sold to Mayagi's Restaurant in Hollywood, where it was converted to an opentop and used as a vehicle to transport guests. The bus was sold once more to Red Bus Rentals in 2002 but as of 2011 its whereabouts are unknown.

Bus 2930 is somewhat closer to home, and was last spotted in 2004 in Lille, France, where it was being used by JLM film productions.

Bus 2816, which appeared in 'The Prize', is now in Budapest, Hungary, owned by Cervimp Ltd, where it is being used to advertise beer, and bus 2916, a background vehicle seen in 'Olive's Divorce' is another export, and as of 2004 resides in Hawaii.

There are, sadly, casualties. The bus driven around by Stan in 'Christmas Duty' (2885 - WNO973F) was sold to Stagecoach in Perth, who scrapped it in 1988. Bus 2743 (EOO585) was last seen in 1978, and bus 2885 (WNO973F) was last seen in 1985 - both are likely to have since been scrapped.

The coach, which featured in 'Private Hire' (YTW538F), is also likely to have been scrapped in the late 1970s.

Other Vehicles - Arthur's Bike

Another key vehicle in *On the Buses* was Arthur's motorbike and sidecar combination, a 1951 BSA M21 model, registration JVB 54, a vehicle, which also cropped up in several episodes of Dad's Army. The motorbike belongs to the BSA owner's club today.

Arthur's bike first appears in the Series Two *On the Buses* episode 'The Used Combination' and is a frequent fixture for the remainder of the series, and the films. But oddly, Michael Robbins, who played Arthur, didn't even have a driving licence.

"He had never learnt to drive," explained Michael's widow, Hal Dyer. "We always took taxis or trains, as he didn't have a car. Michael is often seen driving in *On the Buses*, but that was, I imagine, just a double doing the driving, and a close up of him wearing the helmet. If he ever did drive the bike, I imagine poor Anna Karen in the sidecar would have been terrified."

Lovely Pair of Bristols

But Anna was brave. "I usually did my own stunts," she explains. "It was always me in the sidecar, and a stuntman driving it in the helmet and goggles, as Michael couldn't drive."

It was, perhaps, a wise choice not to get Michael to drive in *On the Buses*. The only occasion he did drive a vehicle in a production nearly ended in havoc. "He did this film called *Looking Glass War*," Hal explained. "He had to drive this lorry in Germany, following a gang of 200 cyclists. The lorry was fitted with air brakes and a few safety features, but he still drove it into a ditch."

6

The 74 Episodes

A total of more than thirty-five hours' worth of *On the Buses* was created by LWT between 1969 and 1973, turning the show into the franchise's highest ranking and most successful comedy product to date. This chapter explains a short summary of each episode, with frequent recollections from the cast, writers, and studio crew, interesting tales from behind the cameras, extracts from Reg Varney's diaries, plus details of filming locations, and errors and continuity mistakes that sneaked into the final edit.

Full episode cast:
Series One: Reg Varney, Bob Grant, Stephen Lewis, Michael Robbins, Anna Karen, Cicely Courtneidge.
Series Two - Series Six: Reg Varney, Bob Grant, Stephen Lewis, Michael Robbins, Anna Karen, Doris Hare
Series Seven (episodes 1-7): Reg Varney, Bob Grant, Stephen Lewis, Anna Karen, Doris Hare
Series Seven (episode 8-13): Bob Grant, Stephen Lewis, Anna Karen, Doris Hare

Unless otherwise stated, all episodes written by Ronald Wolfe and Ronald Chesney.

The 74 Episodes

Series One

The Early Shift
Series 1, Episode 1, Broadcast Friday 28th February 1969.

With: John M. East (Lofty), Rudolph Walker (George), Fraser Kerr (Interviewer), Kevin Moore (Camerman), Michael Slater (Soundman).

When Blakey changes the shifts at the depot, and Stan gets put on the early morning buses, Jack organises a strike. Stan gets himself on the news, and Mum delivers the tea.

Chortle Rating: As the debut episode it has a tendency to come across as quite stilted and uneasy, however the comedy soon develops with positive results. 8/10

Whoopsies: Mum puts a cooked string of sausages in Stan's flask for his lunch. When he takes them out later, they are separated into individual sausages.

Titbits: This is the first episode of *On the Buses*, and it is clear the characters are yet to be fully developed and moulded. Blakey's mannerisms aren't as exaggerated as in later episodes while Jack is conscious of time keeping!

The New Conductor
Alternate Title: Iris
Series 1, Episode 2, Broadcast Friday 7th March 1969
With: Gwendolyn Watts (Iris)

Stan is anxious at the thought of a new conductor on his

bus, but when he sees he has been put on shift with top clippie crumpet, Iris, his opinions change. Alas, Iris is not as sweet as she first appears...

Chortle Rating: Some good work from Gwendolyn Watts. 9/10.

Titbits: Gwendolyn Watts plays Iris. She later went on to appear as Joan Booth in the pilot episode of Love thy Neighbour in 1972, a programme also directed by On the Buses producer Stuart Allen.

Olive Takes A Trip
Series 1, Episode 3, Broadcast Friday 14th March 1969
With: Terry Duggan (Passenger), Geoffrey Denton (Old Gentleman), Michael Slater (Passenger)

When Olive takes a job as a clippie, Stan is horrified. His anguish is made worse when his sister is put on his bus, holding up the journey all day. The reason - Olive suffers from travel sickness. Blakey is flabbergasted, but Stan has an excuse ready and waiting.

Chortle Rating: Nice to have some attention focused on Olive for the first time, as her character isn't a major player in preceding episodes. 8/10

Recollections: "Terry Duggan, [who plays the irate bus passenger in this episode] was a frequent support actor we used in the show. If ever there was any extra part or role, Terry got it. He was married to Anna Karen, who played Olive. They were usually quite small parts, and anyone could have done it really, but we always liked to give it to Terry, he was versatile at what he did." - Ronald Wolfe

The 74 Episodes

Bus Driver's Stomach
Series 1, Episode 4, Broadcast Friday 21st March 1969
With: Richard Caldicot (Doctor Clark), Arthur Lovegrove (Harry), Nosher Powell (Bert)

Oily chips in the canteen and sitting in the cab all day aren't helping Stan's digestion. He has diagnosed himself with a case of bus driver's stomach, but when Blakey announces a forthcoming medical, there is a frantic race to get Butler fit again.

Chortle Rating: Canteen chips appear appetising. 9/10

Whoopsies: Stan is shown to get a puncture in his rubber ring during the location footage of this episode. Jack suggests they can get him a spare, and then boards the bus and rings the bell, however the sound of the bus bell is heard long before Jack presses it.

The New Inspector
Series 1, Episode 5, Broadcast Friday 28th March 1969
With: Doreen Herrington (Clippie), Valerie Newbold (Jenny), Arnold Peters (Manager)

In need of some extra money, Stan is awarded his Inspector's pencils and takes up promotion at the depot, disgusting his work-shy friends, and alienating himself from the rest of the bus crews. Thankfully, his promotion doesn't last long.

Chortle Rating: Jack's opposition to his 'friend's' new job is somewhat concerning. 8/10.

Whoospies: Stan's height is mentioned in this episode to be "5' 7" with his cap on", yet a few series later in "Radio Control", this changes to "5' 2" in me socks."

On Location: The outdoor scenes of Stan as an Inspector were filmed outside Gordon Hill train station, near Enfield, Middlesex. This was a few streets away from Lavender Hill Cemetery, which doubled as the Cemetery Gates in later episodes.

The Canteen
Series 1, Episode 6, Broadcast Friday 4th April 1969
With: Shiranee Fullerton (Mrs Sharma), Nosher Powell (Bert), Mohammad Shamsi (Mr Sharma)

After kicking up a stink about the poor canteen facilities, Stan is charged with improving it. Following a failed attempt at staffing the eatery with an able chef, he ends up getting Mum and Olive in the canteen kitchen. Sadly, his poor maths means he is at a loss on each meal...

Chortle Rating: Some good visual comedy in the way Stan and Jack attempt to cool down post-curry, although stagnant stream water may be less beneficial in the long term. 9/10.

Titbits: The canteen scene in this episode, with Olive's errors in lighting stoves, was reworked into the 1971 On the Buses film.

The Darts Match
Series 1, Episode 7, Broadcast Friday 11th April 1969
With: Valerie Newbold (Jenny), Gwendolyn Watts (Iris)

Stan and Jack challenge the female staff to a darts match, following an argument over the usage of the canteen dart-

A view from behind the camera during the dress rehearsal of 'The Kid's Outing'.
Notice how Doris still has curlers in her hair!

Top: Reg Varney reads through the script of *Holiday On the Buses* at Tony Young's house (the manager's house in the film). Bottom Left: Outside the property with Tony and Ann Young. Bottom Right: A clipping from a local paper advertising for extras for the film.

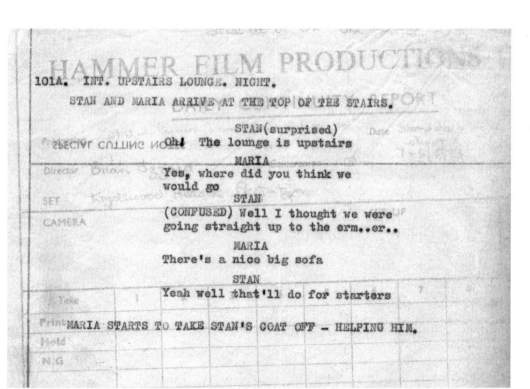

HAMMER FILM PRODUCTIONS

101A. INT. UPSTAIRS LOUNGE. NIGHT.

STAN AND MARIA ARRIVE AT THE TOP OF THE STAIRS.

                    STAN(surprised)
          Oh! The lounge is upstairs

                    MARIA
          Yes, where did you think we
          would go

                    STAN
          (CONFUSED) Well I thought we were
          going straight up to the erm..er..

                    MARIA
          There's a nice big sofa

                    STAN
          Yeah well that'll do for starters

MARIA STARTS TO TAKE STAN'S COAT OFF - HELPING HIM.

Above: A Hammer script sheet from *Holiday On the Buses,*.
Below: A still from the first *On the Buses* film with Pat Coombs.

Above: Anna Karen splashes about in the swimming pool in preparation for the infamous *Holiday On the Buses* 'lost bikini' scene.

Bob Grant during his army service days at Kinmel Camp, Ryhl.
Above: Play it again, Bob. Grant brushes up on the recorder. (photo October 1952)
Below: Bob does some gardening (photo June 1952)

Above: The gang assemble for a photoshoot for the *On the Buses* film.
Below: Olive and Arthur share some quality time together - Series One of *On the Buses*, 1969

Above: Blakey talks to his foam-filled hat after a take in *Mutiny On the Buses*
Below: Reg goes ape, the chimp from Windsor Safari Park visits Elstree Studios to record the studio scenes of *Mutiny On the Buses*.

A model clippie - Anna Karen as the newly divorced Olive, who was given a job at the depot in the Seventh Series of *On the Buses* after Arthur left.

Image credits: P1 Alan Hunter-Craig, P2 Tony Young, P3 Tony Young/Jeanne Varney, P4 Anna Karen, P5 David Dederick, P6 Anna Karen, P7 Jeanne Varney, P8 Anna Karen board. Stan is convinced that he will win, but when Iris starts using her charm to dilute his practice sessions, he is far from match fit on the big night.

Chortle Rating: Funny with a subtle hint of sexism. 9/10

Series Two

Family Flu

Series 2, Episode 1, Broadcast Saturday 31st May 1969
No credited support cast

With Arthur, Olive and Mum all infected with the flu, Jack has the bright idea of shipping the Butler's off to Aunt Maud, leaving the house empty for him and Stan to take some crumpet back to. Alas, the flu is catching...

Chortle Rating: Tarzan of the buses! - 9/10

Whoopsies: In the opening titles, Anna Karen's surname is spelt incorrectly as "Karan."

Whoopsies: When Stan is talking to the baby in the pram at the start of the episode, a boom microphone can be seen in shot on the left of the pram.

Titbits: This was Doris Hare's first appearance as Mum.

Recollections: "Cicely was very good at mum, as was Doris, but the producers thought she wasn't suited for television. I don't really think many people noticed the change anyway!" - Anna Karen.

Filming Locations: The house used for filming in this episode was on Selwyn Road, Willesden. The cooling towers of the now defunct Taylor's Lane power station can be seen in several shots. In later episodes, another house, further up Selwyn road was also used for exterior location filming.

The 74 Episodes

The Used Combination
Series 2, Episode 2, Broadcast Saturday 7th June 1969
No credited support cast

Arthur is conned into buying a wreck of a motorcycle. Out on the road, it predictably breaks down, leaving Stan to get it towed home with the use of a Luxton bus. But Blakey is on the war-path and rumbles his plan...

Chortle Rating: Some strong pieces of comedy dialogue. - 8/10

Whoopsies: A dog can be seen running up to Jack in the location footage of this episode. Bob Grant doesn't react to it and keeps in character.

On Location: Location footage for this episode was filmed on East Brent Lane near Wembley, with the bike breaking down on Oldborough Lane, past the junction of Shelley Gardens in Brent.

Self Defence
Series 2, Episode 3, Broadcast Saturday 14th June 1969
With: Avril Gaynor (Joyce), Ursula Mohan (Liz)

After being attacked on the late night bus, Stan and Jack attend self-defence classes at the depot, run by Blakey. Jack seizes the opportunity for a fumble with the clippies on the crash mat, but it seems they are more proficient at self-defence than he is...

Chortle Rating: Good slap-stick humour. - 9/10

Recollections: "Self Defence was my first episode, I hadn't done much television before, I'd done a lot of classical theatre, so On the Buses was a bit of a shock to do. I remember at the time I'd just got a new agent, and went to a general audition for the part at LWT. I had seen a little bit of the first series, but not too much, my viewing habits were rather irregular as I was doing theatre a lot, but it looked fun and I enjoyed the few parts I'd seen. I remember being so pleased with this episode once I'd finished it; I just had a great laugh doing it.

Something which terrified me was the way the warm-up man introduced all the cast at the start of the episode. This was my first time doing a programme in front of an audience, so I hadn't experienced it before. I was so shocked I had no idea what to say. I nearly died. I think it was Ronald Chesney who did them, and Terry Duggan did lots too, he was very good." - Ursula Mohan (Liz).

Recollections: "I did judo and I was with a stunt agent. The producers wanted a pretty young thing with big bosoms, they couldn't get away with that these days, but that's how I was cast. I don't remember much of my time on the show, it was a fun thing to do, I liked Stephen I'm friends still with Anna Karen. I had to judo tackle Bob Grant, but they may have used a stunt double for him, I can't remember really but they used stunt doubles a lot in those days. I have seen this episode since and I'm actually very embarrassed by it, I think my ballet danc-ing background came through a bit, but I'm not too proud of it, it wasn't the best. At the time I was in a play in Great Yarmouth with Jack Douglas, and just before *On the Buses* I was in Rome.

One thing I do remember is having to thumb a lift back from Rome, I got a last minute flight on a South African airlines jet stopping off in Italy, I'd just come from an end of show party and was clambering up the stairs of the plane at 2am in this yellow trouser suit, got back to London in the morning and went direct to Stonebridge Park for rehearsals!". - Avril Gaynor (Joyce).

The 74 Episodes

Aunt Maud
Series 2, Episode 4, Broadcast Saturday 21st June 1969
With: Betty Hare (Maud)

Mum's sister, Maud, is visiting the Butler household meaning sleeping arrangements are changed, with Stan bunking in with Arthur and getting a sleepless night - not only because his brother-in-law mistakes him for Olive.

Chortle Rating: A good laugh. - 9/10

Titbits: Aunt Maud is played by Betty Hare, Doris Hare's real-life sister. Aunt Maud's dog actually belonged to Anna Karen.

Titbits: In the final scene of this episode, Stan drives the bus with Maud's dog on his lap. However, this created an optical illusion. "I had this great big dog on my knee," Reg Varney recalled in a 1990 interview. "I was driving out of the depot, and two old ladies were walking past, and they did a double take at me and cried 'Blimey, there's a dog driving that bus!'"

Late Again
Series 2, Episode 5, Broadcast Satuday 28th June 1969
With: Sue Walker (Ada) Kate Williams (Doreen)

Stan has been dating Doreen, but his late-night rendezvous are causing problems to his domestic life. In the mornings, Stan sleeps right through his alarm clock, but manages to wake up the rest of the house. Arthur takes action. Stan is late. Blakey is fuming... and Jack pinches Butler's bird.

Chortle Rating: Once again, Jack's actions don't seem very courteous to Stan. - 8/10

Whoopsies: After damage to the original recording tapes, all copies of this episode have a scene missing. Arthur wakes up Stan to complain about the alarm clock noise, and the tape jumps to see Stan out of bed on the other side of the room delivering the line, "Don't be daft, I couldn't find them", indicating a preceding line has been cut out. Blemishes and tape ghosting are also clear. It is most likely that archivists have cut out the damaged section at some point after this episode aired.

Recollections: "I didn't know any of the writers or producers of On the Buses before I appeared in it, so I would have done just a general audition for the part. I did know Anna Karen though, I hadn't worked with her, but we had become friends. I was very lucky with my career, I'd always wanted to be an actress, and I attended the East 15 Theatre School, did a few pantomimes and I think my first television work was Dixon of Dock Green. I had seen On the Buses and I enjoyed watching it; there were a lot of good sitcoms out at that time. I recall being a clippie in one episode, which I believe was the first one and they called me back for another episode later. I'd need to watch the episodes back to remember more; I haven't seen them since they went out" - Kate Williams (Doreen).

Bon Voyage
Series 2, Episode 6, Broadcast Saturday 5th July 1969
With: Patrick Connor (Nobby Clark) Sally Douglas (Eileen)
Dracula poster designed by Terry Griffiths

With their busmen's holiday forthcoming, Stan and Jack attempt to get a head start on the local bronzed lotharios in Spain, and go sunbathing at the cemetery gates. Predictably, things don't go to plan...

The 74 Episodes

Chortle Rating: The cemetery scenes are brilliant. - 9/10

On Location: The cemetery gates scenes were filmed at Lavender Hill Cemetery in Enfield.

Series Three

First Aid

Series 3, Episode 1, Broadcast Friday 2nd January 1970
With: Ruth Kettlewell (Nurse), Suzanne Vasey (Rose)

Blakey catches Butler and Harper skiving at the Cemetery Gates. Halfway though complaining, he slips on their lunch and injures his leg. After a display of ineptitude surrounding first aid, Blakey insists all busmen learn the skill - in their own time...

Chortle Rating: A nice start to the new series. 9/10

Titbits: This is the first episode Blakey says "I 'ate You Butler" - a phrase that would become most associated with the series.

Whoopsies: At the Cemetery Gates, Stan changes the bus blind to display "depot", yet when the bus arrives in the depot, the blind reads "service".

Recollections: "We had massive lectures about moving into colour. We were told how we couldn't have tomato sauce bottles on the table, or anything where colours were vivid, as it would bleed, and we had to look out for stripes, which could potentially strobe on camera. For them, everything was a problem, they'd rather have just forgotten the idea and stayed in black and white!" - Howard Ross (Director)

Reg's Remarks: "Episode One of *On the Buses* transmission 8.30pm. Francis Bennet and John to dinner at Veraswamis, time to be arranged" - Diary Extract; Friday 2nd January, 1970.

The Cistern

Series 3, Episode 2, Broadcast Friday 9th January 1970
With: Terry Duggan (Shopkeeper)

The Butler's bog is on its last legs, so the family spends the day looking around Sankey's plumbing shop to buy a replacement. Alas, back home, Mum's low level loo promotes problems with the high level cistern, and wide level door, causing everybody to venture next door to annoy a none too happy Jack.

Chortle Rating: Some brilliant toilet related comedy - a favourite episode. 10/10

Whoopsies: Blakey orders the toilet off the bus, and Jack jokes about it being a large eggcup. Blakey says; "I'd like to see a bird that could fill an egg with that" instead of the scripted "I'd like to see a bird that could fill an eggcup like that."

Whoopsies: Watch out for the exceptionally wobbly walls in the majority of the bathroom scenes.

Being Chalkie

Glenn Whitter played the character of bus conductor Chalkie in several episodes between 1970 and 1972, both as a credited actor with lines, and an occasional background extra as a passenger or just a walk-on in the depot scenes.

"I was cast in *On the Buses* through my agent," explained Glenn. "I really enjoyed the fun of the filming, and a little socialising outside the show, to be honest I would have to watch all the episodes back again to jog the memory on everything."

These days, the sight of a black actor playing a character called Chalkie, deliberately named to provoke comedy from the issue of race, usually comes as the first example TV critics use to criticise the apparent prejudice in period television, but for Glenn it was never even a remote problem. "For me it made things easier - after all we were doing a comedy and at that time I thought you probably shouldn't read too much into it. I didn't have any problems in that sense, neither then nor now."

In series seven of *On the Buses*, a new actor, Jules Walters takes over as Chalkie, as Glenn was out of the country at the time; "I was in Jamaica," he explained. These days, Whitter has left the acting world to open his own jazz bar on the island, putting "family and a change of course" as the reason for the new way of life.

Titbits: Glenn Whitter, who usually played conductor Chalkie, doubles as a bus passenger when the Butlers board with the toilet.

Recollections: "My husband Terry was in quite a few episodes, he played the toilet shop owner in this one, and he was a passenger in others and a taxi driver in the pets episode. He became well known by the producer so he got cast quite a lot." - Anna Karen

The Inspector's Niece
Series 3, Episode 3, Broadcast Friday 16th January 1970
With: Parnell McGarry (Trainee Clippie), Madeline Mills (Sally)

Stan and Jack are lusting after Sally, a new clippie at the depot. The girl triggers a personality change in the pair, with Stan rushing home for a shave and change of clothes, and Jack opting for flowery shirts and an Audrey Hepburn cigarette holder.

Both compete ferociously for Sally, until they realise the identity of her uncle...

Chortle Rating: Conflict between Stan and Jack is amusing. 9/10

Whoopsies: Doris Hare fluffs a line. She tells Arthur "Don't eat that fork with that fork".

Brew It Yourself
Series 3, Episode 4, Broadcast Friday 23rd January 1970
With: Sally Douglas (Eileen), Glen Whitter (Chalkie)

Beer at home means Davenports - and Stan is convinced he too will become the home beer king. After fermenting his creation in a bucket wrapped in Arthur's eiderdown, the con-

Keep it In the family

Doris Hare got her family in on the act when it came to casting additional guest artists for *On the Buses*. Coming from a theatrical family, her sisters were an obvious choice, and Doris kept it in the family on several occasions. Firstly, her sister, Betty Hare, played Mum's on-screen sister Aunt Maud in the aptly named Series Two episode 'Aunt Maud'. The second Hare sister, who appeared regularly in series three as canteen waitress Winnie, was Winifred Braemer. Winifred also appeared alongside sister Doris in *Confessions of Holiday Camp* in 1977.

coction is ready for a sample, with blinding results. The beer has a strange effect on the Butlers... as well as the varnish on the dining room table.

Chortle Rating: *On the Buses* at its best. 10/10

Recollections: "This was one of Dad's favourite episodes, he always liked the scene where he walks around the depot drunk!" - Jeanne Varney (Reg Varney's daughter)

Reg Remarks: "Read-through of episode four, Station House, Wembley, 10am. VTR of *On the Buses* 2pm, in the tv studio 5pm-9pm" - Diary Extract, Friday 9th January 1970.

Titbits: Due to popular demand, this episode was repeated on Friday 3rd April 1970, after the rest of the series had finished.

Busmen's Perks
Series 3, Episode 5, Broadcast Friday 30th January 1970
With: Lynn Dalby (Janet), Norman Mitchell (Nobby)

Arthur and Olive's bedroom is in dire need of redecoration, and faced with a large bill, Stan steps in with an offer of re-painting. There is a choice of colours - 'Luxton Lodekka Green' or 'Canteen Cream'. Predictably, both such colours will be liberated by Stan from the depot's paint workshop - part of the perks of being a busman. What the manager does, he can too. That's the theory anyway...

Chortle Rating: Great work from Norman Mitchell as Nobby. 9/10

Titbits: Part of this episode was recycled for a scene in *Holiday On the Buses,* with Olive padding around the room and leaving handprints on freshly painted walls.

Whoopsies: When Stan puts his hand on the wall to check if it is dry, it is fleetingly possible to see that his hand has already been painted yellow to provide the effect.

Titbits: In the Series Two episode 'Aunt Maud', Arthur insisted he always slept on the left hand side of the bed, yet in this episode he can be seen dozing on the right.

The Snake
Series 3, Episode 6, Broadcast Friday 6th February 1970
With: Austin Baptiste (Tabla Player), Ishaq Bux (Ahmed), Vemu Makunda (Vina Player), Julie Mendez (Fatima)

After lecherously lusting over snake dancer Fatima at the Indian busmen's social, Jack manages to get a date with her. But there is one unwelcome guest, and the only person who can possibly snake-sit is Stan, who is left with the pet in a washing basket. But telling Stan about the python seems to have slipped Jack's mind...

Chortle Rating: A little disjointed, especially the sudden rearrangement of the rooms in the Butler house, but fun none the less. 8/10

Recollections: "We often had animals in the series, and the producers liked to get as much from the cast as they could; they used my dogs sometimes. The snake in this episode belonged to Julie Mendez, who played Fatima." - Anna Karen

Recollections: "This was havoc in rehearsals, as the snake got loose in the studio. I don't know how much of it was the owner playing games, but I remember it wriggling around on the floor, and it certainly startled the ladies!" - Howard Ross (Director)

Titbits: There is a continuity issue in this episode. The Butlers hide from the snake in the bathroom and looking through the keyhole, they see it enter another room. Stan says, "It's gone in the loo." But there is only one toilet in the household.

Whoopsies: The shot looking through the keyhole should depict the wall directly outside the room the Butlers are in (the bathroom), yet it shows Mum's room, which is located to the right of the bathroom, further down the hall. From the perspective they look out of the keyhole from, it would be impossible to see the room the snake is shown to be in.

Reg Remarks: "Filming location of *On the Buses*, read-through of episode six, Station House, Wembley, 10am." - Diary Extract, Wednesday 28th January 1970.

Mum's Last Fling
Series 3, Episode 7, Broadcast Friday 13th February 1970
With: Eunice Black (Traffic Warden), Tommy Godfrey (Wilfred Phillips), Frank Littlewords (Commissionaire)

Mum has been acting strangely, and it soon transpires there is a man behind her actions, Wilfred, a colleague of Stan's at the depot. With Mum tarting herself up with a fun wig and going out on the town nightly, Stan and Arthur are left with the household chores. Mum wants to marry Wilfred, but there is one member of his family that may object... his wife.

Chortle Rating: One of the best. 10/10

Titbits: Mum's fun wig scene was used again in *Holiday On the Buses*, together with the exact same line "Just because there's snow on the roof, doesn't mean the fire's gone out."

Reg Remarks: "Read through of episode seven of *On the Buses*, Station House, Wembley, 10am. Take car to Graham's for servicing and cleaning of upholstery" - Diary Extract, Friday 6th February 1970.

Radio Control
Series 3, Episode 8, Broadcast Friday 20th February 1970
With: Patricia Clapton (Edna), Ursula Mohan (Joyce), Fraser Kerr (Pilot), Valerie Newbold (Radio Girl)

Blakey, in his infinite wisdom, has decided that each bus will have radio controls fitted, allowing them to keep in constant contact with the depot. Stan and Jack are far from happy being under the close control of Blakey. Thankfully, Blakey is soon to withdraw his bright idea, after an unfortunate incident with a bus and a bridge.

Chortle Rating: A brilliant episode. 9/10

Recollections: "I forget how we did this, but I think we just made a damaged roof out of wood and put it on top of the bus to make it look like it had been crushed by the bridge, the carpenters were very talented at doing things like that." - Alan Hunter-Craig (Designer)

Whoopsies: Before the location footage of the bus on the road, the studio shot stays on Joyce and Edna for too long, and the actresses can be seen covering themselves in talcum powder in preparation for the post-bridge scene where they supposedly get up off the floor covered in dust.

Recollections: "I hadn't done much comedy before I did *On the Buses*, and it was wonderful to do something different. I had done a fair bit of work with Warren Mitchell before. He had helped me since drama school and kept trying to get me into *Til Death Us Do Part* as his daughter. Reg Varney was such a great teacher, he taught me an awful lot. We had a big party after the episode and Reg met my husband, who was a writer. Reg read a lot so they both disappeared for a while, and came back laughing saying I was a terrific actress and I 'should put in something good.' I think though, out of everything I've done, *On the Buses* was the happiest show I'd ever worked on.

"I recall this episode 'Radio Control', I had to get in the cab and get kissed by Reg. He was a lovely man, he bought me lunch every day and always told me how his wife didn't understand him. It was quite sweet really. I also remember we did location work, which was about two months before the episode was filmed. We had to pretend the bus had crashed and get up off the floor covered in dust. One thing I remember was how nice Ursula Mohan was to work with. I was given a mini-skirt which was massive and went down to my ankles, and as Ursula was taller than me she immediately suggested we swap. She was a lovely person." - Patricia Clapton (Edna)

Recollections: "I remember this one, going out on the bus and getting it stuck under a bridge. Most of the shots of the bus was done without us, but any location we did do were all around Stonebridge park in Wembley. Usually all the actors would be taken in a car, or a mini-van if there were a lot of us, we never travelled with the crew and equipment though. Everything was low budget, and it felt low budget, but it was a still a very happy show to be on. And yes, I do remember throwing the dust around in this episode!" - Ursula Mohan (Joyce).

Foggy Night
Series 3, Episode 9, Broadcast Friday 27th February 1970
With: Katherine Page (The Woman Passenger), Peter Brady (Disc Jockey)

Blakey puts Stan and Jack on the worst bus route in the depot, the number 14, running right through the countryside for two hours in the bitter cold. The bus does, however, pass Aunt Maud's house, so the rest of the Butler family take a journey to see her. On the way back, through thick fog, the bus gets marooned with Blakey, Jack and the Butlers stranded in the middle of nowhere, with only a cow and knitting for company.

Chortle Rating: Putting six strong characters together in a confined space for thirty minutes makes this episode an excellent watch. 9/10

Titbits: Shots of the bus travelling through the fog were shot in an empty studio without an audience, the thick dry ice from the industrial smoke machines would have caused complaints from them.

Reg Remarks: "Read through of episode nine, Station House, Wembley, 10am. The two Kens golf cancelled" - Diary Extract, Wednesday 18th February 1970.

The New Uniforms
Series 3, Episode 10, Broadcast Friday 6th March 1970
With: Elyse Clare (Clippie), Pauline Cunningham (Birgit), Yutta Stensgaart (Inga), Glen Whitter (Chalkie)

As the scruffiest, dirtiest pair of lecherous layabouts in the depot, Jack and Stan are chosen as guinea pigs for the new company uniform. The sharp cut, silver-grey ensemble doesn't appeal to the rest of the busmen, but it certainly catches the eyes of some Swedish crumpet, and it looks like Butler and Harper are in for a Smörgåsbord.

Chortle Rating: A very strong episode, another favourite. 10/10

Titbits: Bob Grant forgets his cue at the start of this episode, during the discussion with Blakey about Stan sleeping in his uniform. The line "Only when he's driving" is only prompted when Reg Varney looks at him tentatively and discreetly nudges him.

Recollections: "We actually had to stop filming this episode, because the audience laughter was so loud, they were really in hysterics. It was in the breakfast scene in the house, and Arthur was complaining that Stan got bigger portions than him. He said something like "Why is my sausage smaller than his?" and Reg said something like "Because yours is bent!" And that got one of the biggest laughs in the whole series." - Ronald Chesney.

Going Steady

Series 3, Episode 11, Broadcast Friday 13th March 1970
With: Madeline Mills (Sally)

Stan has been dating Sally, a clippie at the depot, who also happens to be Blakey's niece. The Inspector is determined to put a halt to the relationship, so Stan invites him round for tea that evening to try and sweeten his view. However over tea and light refreshments, the knives are drawn on all sides as Mum defends her son, Arthur insults Olive, Sally insults Mum's baking, Blakey moans at Stan, and Stan sees his girlfriend's true colours.

Chortle Rating: The photo of Blakey's sister always raises a smile. 9/10

Titbits: This was one of the very few episodes that continued from a previous programme. Sally is first introduced earlier in Series Three, in the episode 'The Inspector's Niece'.

Titbits: When it came to finding a suitable picture of baby Stan for the episode (complete with the birthmark on his bottom) director Stuart Allen came to the rescue. The photo, which ended up being used on screen to represent Stan as a toddler is not of Reg Varney, but Allen's newborn son, Ben!

Reg Remarks: "Writers Guild Ball, pick up Ronnie and Rose 7pm". - Diary Extract, Thursday 12th March 1970. "Doris's anniversary, 12 o'clock at her house." - Diary Extract, Sunday 15th March 1970.

The Squeeze
Series 3, Episode 12, Broadcast Friday 20th March 1970
With: Mike Carnell (Milkman), Glen Whitter (Chalkie)

In need of money, Arthur is persuaded to part with his cherished motorbike and sidecar. Searching for an interested buyer takes a decidedly long time, but thankfully there is a certain gullible bus inspector who is ripe for coercion to purchase. A test drive follows, as does trouble...

Chortle Rating: Some excellent visual comedy. 9/10

Whoopsies: The motorbike looks different between exterior and studio shots. The position of the racing tape, window seals, and body paint is noticeably different.

Titbits: When Blakey is in the sidecar with the lid down, an audience member can be heard remaking "Look at his face in there."

Reg Remarks: "Filming at Wood Green garage for episode twelve, read through at Station House, 10am. Recording Tuesday at 8pm" - Diary Extract, Monday 2nd March 1970.

On The Make
Series 3, Episode 13, Broadcast Friday 27th March 1970
With: Patricia Clapton (Edna), Ursula Mohan (Joyce - scene cut)

Edna the clippie has been thrown out of her digs and Stan is partly blame for keeping her out at the pub until the early hours. Butler feels that it is his duty to assist his colleague and suggests she rents his front room. Arthur sees through his brother-in-law's generosity with the attractive conductress, and with new Playboy pyjamas and thin silk dressing gown, Stan is easier to see through than ever.

Chortle Rating: Excellent slapstick and brilliant Arthur versus Stan conflict. 9/10

Titbits: Ursula Mohan had scenes recorded for this episode, but they had to be cut to reduce running time. She is, however, still credited in the closing titles, playing the part of clippie

Strip Art

The popular *Beano* comic strip 'The Bash Street Kids' is said to have taken inspiration from *On the Buses* to develop Olive, the canteen tea-lady in the strips. Olive, who is known to be an atrocious cook with thick rimmed glasses and bland shoulder-length hair was first introduced in 1980 - those who spotted the similarities can be easily forgiven!

Joyce.

Recollections: "Coco was my dog in real life, his name was Maxwell. He appeared in a few episodes, and it was better than the producers hiring a dog, as he was so friendly towards people and was great to work with. My husband Terry always used to sit near him to keep him calm. I think the dog actually got more money than me." - Anna Karen.

Recollections: "I played the same character again in this episode, except I had this huge dog with me, with an enormous suitcase as well, so I got dragged around a lot, but the dog was lovely, very friendly. The part itself was marvellous. I did an enormous amount of television around this time, when I was about 28, usually as a tarty mini-skirted girl. I was fairly well known for it and whenever anybody wanted a tarty girl they called my agent. Reg Varney kept trying to get me in the show more, but it doesn't work like that, my friend's husband was chief dreamer-up of *Z Cars*, but he never got his friends in it.

It just amazes me how popular the show is even now, people call me from abroad saying they've seen me. My hairdresser burnt her cooking the other night, as she was too busy laughing at the show. People still love it. It was from the time when comedy was comedy. I've worked with all the comics, Spike Milligan, Tommy Cooper, The Two Ronnies. It was just a wonderful time in television. On the Buses is repeated constantly on television; and they show episodes with me in quite a lot, but I never see any money for it - very naughty - someone's piling it in." - Patricia Clapton (Edna).

Recollections: "I think I had my scenes cut in this episode. That didn't happen often, but the show was a very quick turnaround - it was all done in a week. We'd rehearse a lot and then have it all recorded on the Friday evening I think. It certainly wasn't a thorough show, and it could look a bit choppy sometimes, but that added to the charm.

I 'Ate You Butler! - The Making of On the Buses

"Stuart Allen was a very good director, he was a sweet man and he laughed a lot. He always supported the cast but in general he was just very supportive and forever smiling." - Ursula Mohan (Joyce).

Titbits: Series three of *On the Buses* originally only comprised of ten episodes, but was extended to thirteen. Reg Varney remarks in his diary on Friday 6th March 1970, "*On the Buses* end of series, but now extended another three. Rehearsals for episode eleven 10am Station House, Wembley".

The 74 Episodes

Series Four

Nowhere to Go
Series 4, Episode 1, Broadcast Sunday 27th November 1970
With: Eric Francis (Joe), Ian Gray (Cleaner), Suzanne Heath (Suzy), Ursula Mohan (Edna)

Stan and Jack have dates with top clippie crumpets Suzy and Edna, but have no suitable place for a romantic rendezvous. Thankfully, Stan has managed to send his family out for the day so the house is empty for him and Jack, or at least it should be...

Chortle Rating: Excellent visual slapstick with the motorbike! 9/10

Recollections: "Something that I remember about *On the Buses* is the way Reg Varney always took you aside when you arrived at the studios and told you all his stories, he was such a sweet man and full of tales of his work in variety.

"This particular episode I haven't seen since it was broadcast. My daughter's boyfriend got me some of them on DVD and I can seldom bring myself to watch them as I get embarrassed. Not the acting or the show, just what I was wearing and my hair! It's such a long time ago, it's a different version of me. I could describe it as looking back on old photographs, but ones that move around and talk. It's incredible!" - Ursula Mohan (Edna)

The Canteen Girl
Series 4, Episode 2, Broadcast Sunday 4th December

With: Gaye Brown (Molly), Alan Curtis (Mr Stewart)

Molly has started working in the depot canteen, and Blakey has his eye on her, dreaming of a happy life in the countryside raising chickens. When Butler and Harper get an idea of what his replacement at the depot will be like, they are adamant to put a spoke in the wheel...

Chortle Rating: Excellent guest work from Gaye Brown 9/10

Titbits: Gaye Brown was in a relationship with Bob Grant until he split up with her to date and marry Kim Benwell.

Whoopsies: When Blakey finds Stan and Molly on the bus, Reg fluffs a line and says, "Now come on, Butler" instead of, "Now come on, Blakey."

Dangerous Driving
Alternate Title: Dangerous Living
Series 4, Episode 3, Broadcast Sunday 11th December 1970
With: Eunice Black (Canteen Girl), Derek Carpenter (Joe), Clare Sutcliffe (Pat)

Mum is horrified to read in the paper that bus drivers have shorter lives than bus conductors, as most of their day involves sitting down. Without her son, she would be distraught, and without his income she would be impoverished. A plan is hatched with Arthur to get Stan in shape.

Chortle Rating: Some especially funny domestic scenes. 8/10

Recollections: "This episode was based on a true story. We read in a newspaper that the bus conductors lived longer, as they walking about and going up and down the stairs all day, whereas the drivers were in the cab and got very little exercise - so this episode seemed a good idea." - Ronald Chesney

Recollections: "My agent would have fixed me up for the episode and interview with the casting people. I was doing amateur dramatics at school, and then I appeared in *The Train Set*, and managed to get into television from there. I can remember hardly anything about my work in *On the Buses*. That long hair would have been a wig, my hair was quite short at the time, so they would have fixed me up with a wig. Doris was very nice, so was Reg Varney, I thought he was great in *The Rag Trade*, which Id watched as a kid, so I was quite awestruck to be working with him, I was only 25. I loved *On the Buses* as a show, also *Ours is a Nice House*, they were all very good, well established shows." - Derek Carpenter (Joe).

The Other Woman
Series 4, Episode 4, Broadcast Sunday 18th December 1970
With: Kate Williams (Wendy)

Arthur is spending an inordinate amount of time with Wendy at the social club, leaving Olive distraught. Arthur eventually spends the night elsewhere, but Olive is comforted when she learns that he actually spent the night in his motorbike sidecar, and that Wendy "wouldn't be seen dead with him."

Chortle Rating: Fiddling the dartboard is a brilliant scene. Stan always seemed to have unusual things down his trousers. 9/10

Recollections: "The only thing I can really remember from this episode is standing at the bar in the canteen with Michael Robbins. They would have called me back for this episode as

I'd already appeared in one before; and they also asked me back for *Holiday On the Buses.*

It was *On the Buses* which got me the role in *Love thy Neighbour*, as they were both directed by Stuart Allen. It was originally going to be Gwendolyn Watts in the part, who was also in *On the Buses* at one point, but I think she was ill so I got the call instead. *Love thy Neighbour* was far from politically correct, critics complain about On the Buses but they would never repeat that!" - Kate Williams (Wendy).

Whoopsies: Michael Robbins fluffs a line while talking to Wendy at the start of this episode. He says, "My Butler is a driver here" instead of the scripted, "My brother-in-law is a driver here".

Whoopsies: Reg Varney fluffs a line. Discussing the darts game with Blakey, he says; "You want to take one of your pills, one for the over 45s to 40s."

Christmas Duty
Series 4, Episode 5, Broadcast Sunday 25th December 1970
With: Roger Avon (Policeman), Eunice Black (Clippie), Ursula Mohan (Joyce), Linda Regan (Edna - uncredited)

Blakey delights in putting Stan and Jack on the Christmas Day service, replacing a crew who are ill. Olive is horrified to learn that she will have to delay Christmas dinner until her brother is back from work, but Mum is adamant about eating as a family. She even goes with Olive and Arthur to the bus depot to pick Stan up. At least they have a white Christmas...

Titbits: Industrial action caused by a technician strike means this episode, together with several more in the latter part of Series Four were transmitted in black and white, and no colour versions exist.

Titbits: Linda Regan, who went on to appear walking up the stairs in the opening credits of the first *On the Buses* film, makes an uncredited appearance as Edna in this episode.

Recollections: "I can't remember why I wouldn't have got a credit for the episode, it may have just been because I didn't have any lines. Stuart Allen the director was a very nice man, and something I remember is Reg Varney tickling me when I kissed him under the mistleoe. I worked again with Ursula Mohan in theatre a few years ago, she's a lovely lady." - Linda Regan (Edna)

The L Bus
Series 4, Episode 6, Broadcast Sunday 1st January 1971
With: Olivia Breeze (Janet), John Lyons (Bert), Juel Morrell (Betty), Michael Slater (Mike), Reginald Stewart (Alf)

Arthur and Olive's bed is on its last legs, but thankfully Jack knows of one going cheap. Unfortunately the bed is across the other side of the town, but the L bus at the depot could solve this problem. It's Stan and Jack's turn to take the trainee drivers and clippies out on a round trip, and they are keen to make the best of having an empty bus for the day. Predictably, Blakey is on to them...

Chortle Rating: Great visual comedy. 9/10

Whoopsies: Blakey issues parcel tickets to Stan at the end of the episode. Bert, the trainee driver asks, "Do you want the mattress next to the head-board or spring base" and Blakey fluffs a line by answering, "Spring-board and spring base?!".

The Kids' Outing

Series 7, Episode 7, Broadcast Sunday 10th January 1971

With: Winifred Braemer (Winnie), Doreen Herrington (Eileen), John Lyons (Bert), Sheridan Earl Russell (Harold), Keith Garrod (Child), Kenneth Flynn (Child), Percy Edwards (bird noises)

Stan and Jack are charged with organising the annual depot outing for the district's kiddies. Olive has been helping with the balloons, getting cake stuck in the mouthpiece of most, and Arthur and Mum have been assisting with the catering. The children seem ungrateful for the effort and even turn to sabotage...

Chortle Rating: Not the strongest of episodes, but some laughs. 6/10

Reg Remarks: "Filming at Wood Green for episode seven. Read through for episode ten, Station House, Wembley." - Diary Extract, Tuesday 17th November 1970.

Recollections: "I'm pretty sure these kids came in from Corona Academy for the day, but it was a bit hectic having them all there. Bless them, but they weren't actors, and tended to run wild. They do say never work with children or animals!" - Anna Karen.

Titbits: Sheridan Earl Russell who played Blakey's nephew went on to play Knuckles in the BAFTA-winning children's film, *Bugsy Malone*.

Titbits: Lucy Allen, the daughter of director Stuart Allen, played one of the children on the bus.

Titbits: A scene from this episode was re-worked into 'The Kid', a Series Two episode of the 1976 LWT sitcom *Yus, My*

Dear with Arthur Mullard, and written by Ronald Wolfe and Ronald Chesney. It has a similar plot as this *On the Buses* episode, with a young boy trying to conceal an adult magazine, but the programme's protagonists being blamed for possessing the mucky mag instead.

The Anniversary

Series 4, Episode 8, Broadcast Sunday 17th January 1971
With: Terry Duggan (Passenger)

Time ticks by slowly when you're married to Olive. After what seems like a lifetime, Arthur has only managed ten years with her. But other members of the family see the event as being more momentous, and Aunt Maud has some nice surprises in store, a dog. Unfortunately, Arthur has an allergy...

Chortle Rating: Enjoyable Arthur versus Olive conflict. 9/10

Recollections: "The little poodle in this episode was my dog too, as was the Great Dane in other episodes." - Anna Karen

Reg Remarks: "VTR for episode eight, Station House, Wembley, 10am. Old ladies home in Stepney, 3pm, charity" - Diary Extract, Friday 4th December 1970.

Titbits: This episode, along with the subsequent shows in Series Four, were transmitted in black and white only because of a colour technicians' strike at LWT.

Cover Up

Series 4, Episode 9, Broadcast Sunday 24th January 1971
With: Eric Francis (Joe), Olive Mercer (Woman Passenger)

Working at a bus depot has its perks. When the chairs at chez Butler need re-upholstering, Stan happily pinches the material from the depot stores. It is a pleasant colour, and very durable. After all if it can last the Friday night special, it should have no problems with any of Olive's cooking...

Chortle Rating: Brilliant visual comedy. 9/10

Titbits: London Transport has actually made this episode a reality, and for the last three years, has been selling bespoke furniture covered in their classic bus and tube moquette material.

Safety First
Series 4, Episode 10, Broadcast Sunday 31st January 1971
With: Ruth Holden (Woman Passenger), Juel Morrell (Betty), Michael Slater (Maintenance Man), Gina Warwick (Nurse)

With so many attractive girls around Luxton, it proves too much for Jack to escort the bus out of the depot without his eyes roving. Alas, this time he directs Stan out into the unclear road and the bus has to brake suddenly, causing one passenger with shopping to be less than happy. Blakey introduces a new system to get the buses in and out of the depot, which ends up causing more problems...

Chortle Rating: Blakey's office is a bit flimsy! 9/10

The Lodger
Series 4, Episode 11, Broadcast Sunday 7th February 1971
With: Samantha Birch (Assistant), Winifred Braemer (Win-

nie), Campbell Singer (Mr Nichols)

A new transport manager from the bus depot takes lodgings at the Butlers' house. Mum is delighted to have an increase in the housekeeping money, but when Olive becomes the centre of Mr Nichols' attentions, the lodger has to be given his marching orders.

Chortle Rating: A good laugh. 8/10

Recollections: "This was another episode that was broadcast in black and white because of the technicians' strike at LWT. As far as bringing colour back to episodes, it's possible for an archivist to do that, but I think it would just be too expensive. I don't think it would generate enough money to warrant it." - Howard Ross (Director)

The Injury
Series 4, Episode 12, Broadcast Sunday 14th February 1971
With: Patricia Shakesby (Nurse), Michael Slater (Joe)

Stan is doing some DIY at home, but after a nasty fall in the bath, landing on Olive on the process, he breaks his foot. It will mean he will be off work for weeks without pay, unless he can make good on Jack's suggestion, and pretend he got injured at work. Everything is planned, and a step on the stairs at the depot has been tampered with. Blakey puts his foot in it.

Chortle Rating: Falling on Olive should really be a soft landing... 9/10

Not Tonight
Series 4, Episode 13, Broadcast Sunday 21st February 1971
With: Winifred Braemer (Winnie), Ursula Mohan (Joyce),
Deirdre Costello (Molly), Charlotte Howard (Stella)

Stella, a new clippie at the depot, has caught Stan's eye.
But her sugary smile hides a nasty dark-side and, before long,
she has been bleeding Stan dry of all his money. Using Butler's
dosh for new attire, she has also managed to secure a job in
the manager's office at the depot. Stan is left potless and Mum
is demanding the rent.

Chortle Rating: Poor Stan has been had. 9/10

Tickets Please...

Jack and the other bus conductors issued tickets to passengers with the help of Setright Mk2 ticket machines, which were also loaned from Eastern National buses along with the vehicles used in the show.

Setiright ticket machines, often nick-named "speed ticket machines" because of the quickness of printing and issuing tickets to passengers, were a popular tool with bus companies across the Country. When bus conductors became a less common sight, driver-operated digital 'Wayfarer' machines replaced the Setrights, and these machines can still be seen on most buses today.

The 74 Episodes

Series Five

The Nursery
Series 5, Episode 1, Broadcast Sunday 19th September 1971
With: Ruth Kettlewell (Nurse), Laura Graham (Clippie)

A nursery has been set up at the depot to cater for the clippie's children, and learning that the nurse is looking for an assistant, Stan puts Olive up for the job. But after sitting on her glasses and having to go home for her spare pair, Butler and Harper are left in charge of babies. A bad idea...

Chortle Rating: A good episode to start a new series. 8/10

Whoopsies: A clippie can be seen hiding out of shot behind the bus at the start of this episode, awaiting her cue.

Recollections: "I lived in Worcester at the time, and travelled down to London to do *On the Buses*. The producers had seen my photograph in Spotlight, and phoned my agent. I was very happy to be accepted, as I thought the show was a good comedy. It was amusing, and it was very popular. Reg Varney was so professional, he was an extremely generous, kind man. It was a great pleasure to be working with someone of his calibre. But everyone was very nice.

"It was always interesting to watch the other members of the cast working together. I was young actress, and they were all very strong, hardened performers. I was happy just to watch them from the wings, see them go through the motions, and I learnt from it. Having the audience there was also exciting, it was like being on stage, it was lovely to play to both camera and audience, the best of both worlds." - Laura Graham (Clippie).

Stan's Room
Series 5, Episode 2, Broadcast Sunday 26th September 1971
With: Pat Ashton (Doreen)

Mum can always tell when Stan is trying to sneak a girl upstairs and, as her house is a respectable one, she always puts a stop to it. This attitude forces Stan to move out, and he takes digs at Blakey's house. But even the Inspector is unhappy with Butler turning his spare room into an orgy, and banishes all females from the house. Stan has a plan...

Chortle Rating: Some brilliant conflict in the domestic scenes. 8/10

The Best Man
Series 5, Episode 3, Broadcast Sunday 3rd October 1971
With: Robin Parkinson (Vicar), Sandra Miller (Sally), Hugh Walters (Bill)

Blakey's niece is marrying one of the busmen, much to his annoyance. He is even more agitated when he learns Stan has been charged with being the best man at the wedding. His worries are justified. Stan and Jack manage to get the groom drunk just hours before he is due to walk up the aisle...

Chortle Rating: Brilliant inebriated acting. 9/10

Filming Locations: The church used in this episode was St Mary the Virgin in the village of Denham, near Uxbridge. This same church was also used for the wedding scenes in both *Carry On Matron* and *Carry On Don't Lose Your Head.*

The 74 Episodes

The Inspector's Pets

Series 5, Episode 4, Broadcast Sunday 10th October 1971
With: Don McKillop (Harry), Terry Duggan (Taxi Driver)

Bollards. The bane of a busman's life and Stan has crashed into another one. He needs to sneakily repair the damage to his bus and thankfully Blakey is due to go away for a few days. But the plans fall apart when the Inspector announces his pet-sitter has become unavailable. There is only one solution...

Chortle Rating: Some excellent work from Michael Robbins. 9/10

Whoopsies: Mitzi the dog is supposedly a female, yet in the scene when Arthur brings it home from the pub, Michael Robbins mistakenly calls it "he" for the entire scene. He corrects himself after realising the mistake.

Whoopsies: Blakey bemoans how it took him two days to dig up the worms, but later in the episode he says it took him three days.

The Epidemic

Series 5, Episode 5, Broadcast Sunday 17th October 1971
With: Ruth Kettlewell (Nurse), Sharon Young (Sandra), Cheryl Hall (Eileen), Philip Dunbar (Barman), Keith Norrish (Brian), Eric Kent (extra - uncredited).

Flu is doing the rounds, and revelling in the overtime, Jack and Stan are determined to remain as healthy as they can, getting frequent inoculations from the depot nurse. Alas, on a date with an attractive clippie, Stan starts to feel ill...

Chortle Rating: Very watchable. 7/10

Whoopsies: Mum goes to retrieve a thermometer from the sideboard. Instead of saying, "I'll get the thermometer out" she instead fluffs a line and explains, "I'll just get the temperature out."

The Busmen's Ball
Series 5, Episode 6, Broadcast Sunday 24th October 1971
With: Glen Whitter (Chalkie), Wendy Richard (Elsie)

Blakey is disgusted to learn that Stan and Jack have booked a stripper for the entertainment at the annual busmen's ball. The rest of the Butler family attend the event too, and for once, Olive becomes the centre of attention. It doesn't last...

Chortle Rating: Nice to see Wendy Richard briefly appear as a clippie. 9/10

Titbits: Bob Grant injured the forefinger of his right hand whilst filming this episode. This is evident in later scenes when he can be seen wearing a bandage around it. The dressing is absent at the start of the episode.

Canteen Trouble
Series 5, Episode 7, Broadcast Sunday 31st October 1971
With: Andrea Lawrence (Sally), Fanny Carby (Gladys), Glen Whitter (Chalkie), Luan Peters (Joan)

Stan has been using his friendship with the canteen manageress to get his hands on surplus food from the kitchens. It means that the Butler household can enjoy some meat for once. But Blakey is soon on to Stan's plan, and in an effort to cut the canteen's losses, a stern female ex-prison officer is brought in to replace Suzy. But everyone can be flattered, much to Stan's horror...

Chortle Rating: Great cameo work from Fanny Carby. 8/10

Whoopsies: In the confines of a studio, moving a double decker bus could be very difficult, not to mention dangerous, so the camera operators employed a clever trick. By panning along the side of the bus, it could be made to look like the bus was moving off forwards. However, the idea comes unstuck in this episode, when, just before the commercial break, the shiny wings of the bus clearly reflects the camera, camera operator, and the rest of the studio crew employing this nifty manoeuvre.

The New Nurse
Series 5, Episode 8, Broadcast 7th November 1971
With: Hal Dyer (Mary), Sandra Miller (Sally), Keith Norrish (George)

A new nurse at the depot is in need of accommodation, and moves into the front room of the Butlers' house, much to Arthur's delight. Infatuated with Mary, he takes her out to the pictures and neglects Olive in favour of the nurse's company. But it can't last long, a fact for which Olive is grateful...

Chortle Rating: A favourite. 9/10

Titbits: Hal Dyer, who played the part of the nurse, was Michael Robbins' wife in real life.

Recollections: "The part of the nurse was written especially for me, which was lovely, and I decided to play her as a rather refined Scot. Derrick Goodwin the director was a good friend, and had set this up. I only really got the part because I was married to Michael and I knew all the cast, they were always great fun to work with. Ronnie Wolfe and Ronnie Chesney said I was too posh to be in the show more, they used to laugh and say my boobs weren't big enough." - Hal Dyer (Mary).

Lost Property
Series 5, Episode 9, Broadcast Sunday 14th November 1971
With: Amelia Bayntun (Woman), Bartlett Mullins (Joe)

After Stan and Jack are caught eating a portion of fish and chips left on the bus by a passenger, and the telling evidence of fish bones in the used ticket bin being a giveaway of such culinary misdeeds, Blakey puts in a new rule that all lost property has to be declared. The busmen have a laugh with the rule, purposely leaving dubious objects on board, but when Stan takes home an ostensibly plain envelope home with an evening paper, and mislays the contents, a diamond, the problems really start...

Chortle Rating: Some excellent comedy work from *Carry On* regular Amelia Bayntun. 9/10

Stan's Uniform
Series 5, Episode 10, Broadcast Sunday 21st November 1971
With: Norman Mitchell (Nobby), Brian Grellis (George)

Why do dirty household jobs in your own clothes when the company provide uniform? Stan has been clearing the drains and unblocking the sink in his, and every few years, is reward-ed with a new one. But just days a few days with the new gar-ment, and Stan has an accident with a pot of paint...

Chortle Rating: Accidents happen rather too conveniently, but a good show none the less. 8/10

The Strain
Series 5, Episode 11, Broadcast Sunday 28th November 1971
With: Pat Ashton (Doreen), James Bree (Dr Clark), Nosher Powell (Vic), Keith Norris (Busman)

There are many hobbies and past-times to entertain the idle bus driver, with a particular favourite being a "guess the weight of the clippie" contest. Stan makes a valiant attempt at such an activity, but injures his back in the process and ends up in a medical truss, to Arthur's hysterics.

Chortle Rating: Particularly enjoy the canteen scenes at the start. 9/10

The New Telly
Series 5, Episode 12, Broadcast Sunday 5th December 1971
With: Shirley Steedman (Eileen), David Richardson (George), Keith Norrish (Busman), Peter Cockburn (TV Commentator)

When Stan learns that the TV repair man refused to buy his ancient television in part exchange for a colour set, he goes about selling it to muster the necessary funds. Only one per-son at the depot could be gullible enough to take the clapped out telly off his hands. He is about six feet tall, has a small moustache, and his name starts with a B...

Chortle Rating: Brilliant Blakey versus Stan comedy. 10/10

Vacancy For Inspector

Series 5, Episode 13, Broadcast Sunday 12th December 1971
With: Madeline Mills (Christine), Glen Whitter (Chalkie)
Written by: Bob Grant and Stephen Lewis

As shop steward, Jack is offered the job of assistant Inspector, a novel idea from the management to keep the union on side. Stan doesn't approve of his mate's new post, especially as all of his bad habits are snitched on, and his girlfriend, Christine, ends up in Jack's clutches. After one week, Stan has had enough of Harper's deeds. But fortunately, before long, Jack sees sense, and Blakey gets a battering...

Chortle Rating: Excellent slapstick, especially Blakey getting covered in batter. 9/10

A Thin Time

Series 5, Episode 14, Broadcast Sunday 19th December 1971
With: Alex Marshall (Beryl)
Written by: Bob Grant and Stephen Lewis

In need of a restoration to his manhood, Arthur turns to the Curlytop Corporation, and gets five hairpieces on approval. But approval is non-existent - Stan is the first to mock, followed by Jack and Olive thinks her husband is turning funny. One person is a fan, a clippie at the depot called Beryl. Olive is fretting about losing her husband to her but Arthur just can't keep his hair on...

Chortle Rating: Another favourite. 10/10

Boxing Day Social

Series 5, Episode 15, Broadcast Sunday 26th December 1971
With: Gillian Lind (Mrs Rudge), Helen Fraser (Linda Rudge), Janice Hoy (Beryl), Kenneth Waller (Busman)

Arthur's sister and mother are in Luxton for a festive visit. Jack is smitten by Linda, but Arthur doesn't feel a bus conductor is suitable suitor for his sister and puts a stop to the relationship. However his problems are closer to home than he likes to think, and Stan is the next target in Linda's sights...

Chortle Rating: Brilliant cameo work from Helen Fraser. 8/10

Titbits: This is one of the few comedy roles that support actor Kenneth Waller plays his own age. He famously went on to age-up for the role of Grandad in *Bread* and Old Mr Grace in the eighth series of *Are You Being Served?*

Recollections: "I don't think I have a favourite episode, but I loved doing 'The Cistern', and I liked 'The Boxing Day Social' one too. Michael laughed so much in this that he had to walk off set, the director was very angry with both of us, but he left a bit in and you can see Michael cracking up and me trying to keep a straight face. Then I did a striptease on the table but it was all very well humoured. Olive was always well covered, especially with her chilblains". - Anna Karen

Series Six

No Smoke Without Fire
Series 6, Episode 1, Broadcast Sunday 20th February 1972
With: Pauline Cunningham (Frieda), Mary Land (Suzy), Eunice Black (Gladys)
Written by: Bob Grant and Stephen Lewis

A fire in the paint warehouse leads Blakey to ban all smoking in the bus depot. This sparks an argument between Stan and Jack about who smokes the most, and the pair eventually strikes up a bet. If one catches the other smoking, there is a fiver at stake. Stan is sneaky enough to have a puff on a fag without getting caught, but when he mislays his cigarette in the used ticket bin of the bus, an inferno ensues and guess who gets trapped upstairs...

Chortle Rating: Waste of a bus, but a good episode. 8/10

Recollections: "This episode was a very complicated sequence, as we actually torched a bus. If I recall someone chucked a fag in the ticket bin, and the bus went on fire. I'm not too sure how I shot it, but we had to have two cameras, one on the ground, and we took another one up in a helicopter. Using a helicopter, as well as burning a bus, all out on location, made the episode quite expensive to film, one of the most costly of the series, but nothing in comparison to today. I found some paperwork recently for another show I did, called *Thick as Thieves*, which was made for £9,000 an episode. I don't know how much it costs to make a comedy these days, but in comparison to the stuff we did, it makes the budget for buses look like peanuts." - Derrick Goodwin (Director).

Recollections: "Very expensive is all I can say! That bus went like a bomb, the engine was taken out of it first and we took it to a field and torched it there. It was quite an old bus and we were called vandals for destroying it. In fairness we did smash a lot up. When we usually wanted to ruin a bus though, we had to fake it so a smashed window or dented bumper would just be crepe paper and we'd paint it to look like damage." - Alan Hunter-Craig (Production Designer)

Love Is What You Make It
Series 6, Episode 2, Broadcast Sunday 27th February 1972
With: Jacqui Cook (Clippie), Aubrey Morris (Marriage councillor), Johnny Briggs (Window cleaner)
Written by: George Layton and Jonathan Lynn

Stan has had enough of Olive and Arthur's bickering, and decides to take action. After a failed discussion with a marriage guidance counsellor, he eventually decides to try and make Arthur jealous by letting him find Olive in a passionate embrace with another man. Only one man is daft enough to be roped in...

Chortle Rating: A short appearance by *Corrie's* Johnny Briggs is fun to spot. 8/10

Private Hire
Series 6, Episode 3, Broadcast Sunday 5th March 1972
With: Maurice Bush (Basher), Ursula Mohan (Iris), Mary Maxted (Iris's Mum), Glen Whitter (Chalkie)
Written by: Bob Grant and Stephen Lewis

Gambling losses are taking their toll on Stan's finances, and he ends up borrowing funds from Basher, the toughest tire-changer in the depot. Butler desperately needs to recoup the owed money, to spare the injuries, which will no doubt happen to his bodily functions. He decides to try and make money from his bus. Helping the office receptionist move house is one plan, but another more financially rewarding one is on offer. The plan is made better by Blakey's absence, but Dracula makes a frightening reappearance at the wrong time...

Chortle Rating: Blakey's stunt on the piano is a favourite scene. 9/10

Recollections: "I kept getting asked back for shows, but it was always different characters. I did a stint as Joyce for quite a while, and I think I also did Edna, Iris and Liz; it was hilarious. I was usually a clippie, but in this episode I'd been promoted to the front office, I just remember those white boots and that yellow and black bee-like sweater, that and the big hair.

I think it was this episode we were all out on location and when we paused filming this huge crowd of people suddenly started swarming around Reg, I had never experienced anything like that and it really brought home to me just how popular this show was, and the power of television." - Ursula Mohan (Iris).

Stan's Worst Day
Series 6, Episode 4, Broadcast Sunday 12th March 1972
With: Terry Duggan (Painter), John M. East (Mechanic), Frederick Hall (Manager)
Written by: Bob Grant and Stephen Lewis

Domestic life at home is on the rocks again, so Stan takes a trip down memory lane, recalling when he first met Jack, Blakey's promotion to Inspector, and that fateful encounter between Olive and Arthur...

Chortle Rating: Interesting to see the supposed origins of the Blakey versus Stan Feud. 9/10

Union Trouble
Series 6, Episode 5, Broadcast Sunday 19th March 1975
With: Marcia Ashton (Elsie), Glen Whitter (Chalkie)
Written by: Bob Grant and Stephen Lewis

The staff goes on strike to save the job of Stan's friend in the canteen, but when the other busmen realise they won't be getting paid, it's Stan alone who ends up skipping work until demands are met. Staying the night in the empty depot alone doesn't faze him, but there is a tall menacing figure lurking in the shadows that does...

Chortle Rating: Blakey needs some WD-40 for his squeaky shoes. 8/10

Bye, Bye Blakey
Series 6, Episode 6, Broadcast Sunday 26th March 1972
With: Garfield Morgan (Mr Stilton), Petra Siniawksi (Clippie), Catherine Kessler (Nurse), Nicolette Roeg (Doctor), Philip Dunbar (Bus Driver)
Written by: George Layton and Jonathan Lynn

Stan and Jack overhear Blakey's medical at the depot, and on hearing that "he won't be around for much longer", believe that he is on his last legs. Blakey is, in reality, getting a job elsewhere. It still prompts Butler and Harper to be nice to him on his last few weeks on Earth. However when the truth comes out, nothing changes...

Chortle Rating: Some brilliant domestic scenes with Blakey round for tea! 9/10

The Prize
Series 6, Episode 7, Broadcast Sunday 2nd April 1972
With: Julia Breck (Canteen Girl), Glen Whitter (Chalkie - uncredited)
Written by: George Layton and Jonathan Lynn

Mum has won a holiday for two in the Costa Brava. The only snag is that there are three people baying for the extra place and Arthur, Stan and Olive all try their utmost to get in Mum's good books. Alas, the depot raffle turns out to be a fraud...

Chortle Rating: Best episode of the series. 9/10

Fares Please!

The *On the Buses* popularity means that the series is very often on television, but some production crew feel cheated of royalties. "A friend of mine was telling me how often *On the Buses* was repeated," explained series six director Derrick Goodwin. "It is on five days a week, three or four times a day. But I have never seen one single penny of that. I don't know what contracts we were on, but it must have been a one-off fee, as there have been no more royalty fees since the shows went out. The contracts must have been well stitched up. Either that, or they didn't expect the shows to be re-run."

The lack of repeat fees is a frequent talking point with other members of the *On the Buses* team. "I got a cheque," Ursula Mohan explained. "It was for every On the Buses episode I did from when they put them onto VHS. I got 63p."

Series Seven

Olive's Divorce
Series 7, Episode 1, Broadcast Friday 9th February 1973
    With: Sandra Bryant (Sandra), Sue Bond (Clippie - uncredited)

The day has finally come, and Olive is divorcing Arthur, who has done a runner, leaving only his prunes at the back of the larder. Olive is distraught, but Stan has other girls on his mind, namely Sandra, who he has a date with. Alas, Mum steps in, insisting that Olive spend time with her brother, and Stan has to think on his feet so not to scupper his date. Thankfully, Blakey is free that evening...

Chortle Rating: A little weak, and sad to see the back of Arthur with his dry wit and caustic insults. 5/10

Recollections: "People often found it hard to understand there was a difference between television and real life. When I divorced Arthur, my real husband Terry was out shopping and this woman walked up to him saying 'Ere, you're married to Olive. It's a bloody disgrace her divorcing Arthur.' Neither of us could ever get our head around that!" - Anna Karen

The Perfect Clippie
Series 7, Episode 2, Broadcast Friday 16th February 1973
    With: Frederick Peisley (Doctor), Peter Davidson (Passenger)
    Written by: George Layton and Jonathan Lynn

Without Arthur's income, the family is facing difficult times, so Olive applies for a job on the buses which, amazingly, she gets. Stan and Jack are less than happy when she is put on their bus for training, especially as she begins insisting they work to rule on duty. Olive's pedantry culminates in a revolution at the depot...

Chortle Rating: Olive's rule following is annoying. 7/10

Reg Remarks: "Filming location On the Buses, Dulwich, 6.30am" - Diary Extract, Monday 15th January 1973.

Recollections: "Series Seven had a different set of opening titles, as Michael had left and needed to be cut of them. So they drew this cartoon of us all, and Olive was an enormous fat lump with a lollypop. It wasn't flattering, but it wasn't that hurtful. By that time I was bulletproof!" - Anna Karen.

The Ticket Machine
Series 7, Episode 3, Broadcast Friday 23rd February 1973
With: Michael Sheard (Manager)
Written by: Bob Grant and Stephen Lewis

Mum and Olive have been conned by a magazine which promises to make them rich, becoming sales agents for the company's products. Keen to get their sales started, they buy £50 worth of goods themselves, a guitar, crockery set, and a new dress. They need to try and reclaim their money, and thankfully Jack has a clever scheme on the boil, involving a stolen ticket machine...

Chortle Rating: A fun plot, if not overly farcical. 8/10

The 74 Episodes

The Poster
Series 7, Episode 4, Broadcast Friday 2nd March 1973
With: Kenneth Gilbert (Chemist), Elaine Wells (Assistant), Michael Sheard (Manager), John Crocker (Second Judge), Nick Hobbs (Finalist), Perry Soblosky (Finalist), Folker Henrix (Finalist)
Written by: Wally Malstan and Garry Chambers

Luxton and District are spreading their message of safety and passenger comfort with an advertising campaign, and a contest between all the regional depots begins to find the face of the posters. The winner receives a cash prize. Jack helps Stan improve his appearance with face creams and other enhancing cosmetics, but the only way Butler is destined to win is with a bit of realism...

Chortle Rating: Good slapstick. 8/10

Whoopsies: The 'your face could be here' advertisement for the competition, is clearly the finished poster with Stan's face on it, just blacked out. The position of the arms in the cab proves this.

The Football Match
Series 7, Episode 5, Broadcast Friday 9th March 1973
With: Jules Walters (Chalkie), Bob McNab (Bob), Melanie Jane (Canteen girl), Carol Gilles (Eunice), Jenifer Guy (Iris), Jeanette Wild (Rita), Maxine Casson (Mary)
Written by: Bob Grant and Stephen Lewis

The Luxton Lions are due to play the Basildon Bashers and with the prospect of a fiver to every player on the winning team, Stan and Jack join the squad at the depot. Their confidence is boosted when they discover they are up against an all-women's football team, but for the majority of the game, the Bashers are on the ball...

Chortle Rating: Not the strongest for comedy, indeed rather disjointed in plot. Introducing a supposed football team which has gone unmentioned over the previous four years is odd, but for slapstick this episode is rather amusing, especially Olive's football skills in the closing credits. 8/10

Whoopsies: Blakey books Stan during the football match, but instead of a yellow card, he shows him a red.

On the Omnibuses
Series 7, Episode 6, Broadcast Friday 16th March 1973
With: Lucy Griffiths (Old lady), Paul Dawkins (Manager)
Written by: Bob Grant and Stephen Lewis

An exhibition at the depot to mark the anniversary of the bus company leads Stan to have a dream about what life would be like back then. A Victorian Blakey is even less fun that the current one, and Olive is a suffragette.

Chortle Rating: A loose, weak plot, but some funny farcical period scenes. 8/10

Reg Remarks: Location filming at Slaugham Manor, Sussex, 6.30am" - Diary Extract, Monday 22nd January 1973.

Titbits: This episode uses the most location footage over the entire series, with only the manager's office scenes being filmed in a studio with an audience present.

Whoopsies: Several historical anachronisms appear in this episode. Most famously, lurking behind the fruit stall in the supposed Victorian street, a parked 1971 Morris car can be seen. The front bumper, radiator and headlights are visible. Later in the episode, Olive is chained to the railings, but locking together her chains is a modern padlock.

Filming Locations: This episode was filmed almost entirely on location, around the area of the Bluebell railway in Kent. The period house used was Slaugham Manor.

Goodbye Stan
Series 7, Episode 7, Broadcast Friday 23rd March 1973
With: Jules Walters (Chalkie) John Lyons (Bill)

Mum is in tears when Stan ups sticks and moves away from home. He has secured a better job in the Midlands, working in a car factory. In need of more money to run the house, Mum advertises for a lodger, and ends up having Blakey move in. He is less than happy with the state that Stan has left the place...

Chortle Rating: Reg leaving the series tarnishes the comedy somewhat. 7/10

Hot Water
Series 7, Episode 8, Broadcast Friday 30th March 1973
With: Melanie Jane (Joyce) Michael Sheard (Manager)
Written by: Bob Grant and Stephen Lewis

Blakey is now the lodger at the Butler household and already he is facing problems. The water heater has broken leaving him, Olive and Mum with cold morning baths. Jack comes to the rescue with a collection of spare heating elements, but the Inspector isn't comfortable with their origins...

Chortle Rating: The best episode of the final series. 8/10

Reg Remarks: "Rehearse *On the Buses*, transmission of series seven. Roy Skeggs RE: Buses film" - Diary Extract, Tuesday 30th January 1973.

Recollections: "I didn't go along to the location filming of this episode, but I remember we needed to get a special effects crew in. Burst water tanks and other more visual set-ups always called for a special effects team. They were very good at their job; we had them do all the sparks, explosions, pyrotechnics. They also had the right licences, which we didn't, so they could handle firearms and explosive chemicals." - Alan Hunter-Craig (Set Designer).

The Visit
Series 7, Episode 9, Broadcast Sunday 8th April 1973
With: Pat Nye (Mrs Blake)
Written by: George Layton and Jonathan Lynn

Blakey is overjoyed when his mother announces she is coming for a visit. The pity is that Mrs Blake is one of the nastiest, surliest and selfish women there is, and before long Olive and Mum can see what they have let themselves in for...

Chortle Rating: An irritating, dragging and frustrating episode. 2/10

What The Stars Foretell
Series 7, Episode 10, Broadcast Sunday 15th April 1973
With: Larry Martin (Fred), Sandra Bryant (Sandra), Nina

West (Wendy), Michael Sheard (Manager)
   Written: Bob Grant and Stephen Lewis

Mum and Olive have become facsinated by their horo-scopes, convinced there is truth in astrology. When the tealeaves in their cups show wedding bells, they are both convinced that marriage is around the corner. The lucky suitor? It has to be Blakey!

Chortle Rating: The comedy is becoming very thin at this point, and even Doris Hare in a silly costume and wig isn't enough to redeem it. 4/10

The Allowance
Series 7, Episode 11, Broadcast Sunday 22nd April 1973
   With: Yootha Joyce (Jessie), Michael Sheard (Manager), Claire Davenport (Mrs Webb), Sandra Bryant (Sandra), John Lyons (Sid)
   Written by: Miles Rudge

A new militant clippie, Jessie, is determined to get the girls at the depot an allowance to use the chargeable public toilets on the bus routes. The three tings a tinkle campaign is launched, and Jack, as shop steward, takes up the challenge of getting the management to divvy up. Blakey ends up being given the task of conducting a survey to see exactly how many times a girl needs to powder her nose...

Chortle Rating: The brilliant Yootha Joyce in her pre-Mildred days is the only redeeming feature of this otherwise fairly bland episode. 6/10

Titbits: This episode was a good reunion for some of the cast. Bob Grant, John Lyons and Yootha Joyce had all worked previously at Joan Littlewood's theatre workshop at the start of their careers.

Friends In High Places

Series 7, Episode 12, Broadcast Sunday 29th April
With: Bob Todd (Mr Simpson), Claire Davenport (Mrs Webb), Albert Moses (Alf)
Written by: George Layton and Jonathan Lynn

After a fracas in the canteen, the depot looks for a new cook. Jack suggests Mrs Butler, and she goes along to meet the area manager, Mr Simpson, who it turns out, used to work with mum's late husband, Albert, in a munitions factory during the war. The trip down memory lane leads Mr Simpson to become a family friend, and the Butlers can now boast about being on strong terms with the management. Blakey doesn't like that one bit...

Chortle Rating: Good Blakey versus Jack conflict. 7/10

Recollections: "I had worked with the casting directors before, and they always remember actors who they have introduced to directors, and keep a tab on their work so they can recommend them to other directors when the opportunity comes up. The cast were a wonderful bunch, we thoroughly enjoyed working together, it was fun and we were paid for it. There was this one time I was getting off the bus and slipped and fell flat on my face. I couldn't believe it that they all laughed their guts out and no one asked me if I was OK. I realised that they thought that I did it as a joke. I had no choice but to pretend I was joking, although my leg did hurt." - Albert Moses (Alf).

Gardening Time

Series 7, Episode 13, Broadcast Sunday 6th May 1973

With: Sandra Bryant (Sandra), Michael Shears (Manager), Larry Martin (Fred), Ivor Slater (Policeman), Ernest C Jennings (Rag and bone man), Tiberus Grant (Tibbles)

Written by: Bob Grant and Stephen Lewis

The depot gardening competition is in full swing, and as the only two in the competition, Blakey and Jack go head to head to win the prize. Dirty tactics on both sides ensue, but after a week, both are eager to find out the winner.

Recollections: "If I recall, Bob Grant brought his own cat in for this episode!" - Anna Karen

Chortle Rating: The last episode, it's all quite poignant for a dedicated fan. Alas, it isn't the strongest episode. There were many missed chances here to give *On the Buses* a decent send-off. The only humorous sight is Bob Grant's cat getting a mention in the titles. 6/10

All Star Comedy Carnival

Christmas Special, Broadcast Monday 25th December 1972
Written by: Bob Grant and Stephen Lewis

Filmed as part of ITV's popular Christmas slot *The All Star Comedy Carnival*, a direct competitor to the BBC's *Christmas with the Stars, On the Buses*, together with several other well-loved ITV shows from across the franchise were condensed into bite-sized portions for the viewing pleasure of audiences at home over the festive season.

Popular sitcoms, also including *Father Dear Father, Love thy Neighbour* and *The Fenn Street Gang*, had short five-minute sketches devised and produced for transmission within the festive extravaganza, written by the original writers of each comedy, and usually starring the full cast. The *On the Buses* sketch, written by Series Six writers Bob Grant and Stephen Lewis, involved the gang trying to track down a runaway goose.

Plot

The short sketch revolves around a live goose being found as lost property on Jack's bus. Both Mum and Olive were passengers on the same vehicle, and join the ensuing chase around the bus depot to retrieve the bird. Blakey, as ever, comes off the worst as his hat gets filled with eggs and his face covered in exhaust soot from the bus.

Cast and Crew

The short was created after the Sixth Series of *On the Buses* had ended, meaning that Michael Robbins had already left the series, and was absent from the special edition. Similarly, Reg Varney was missing from this programme, despite not having officially left the main television series - Reg's absence from the short sketch was reportedly due to contractual reasons, with him most likely being preoccupied with his variety show, *The*

Other Reg Varney.

Instead, Larry Martin, who later took up residence in the Seventh Series of On the Buses as driver Bert, indirectly took over Varney's role as the bus driver in the sketch.

Bob Grant, Stephen Lewis, Doris Hare and Anna Karen all reprised their characters.

Technical Details

This wasn't the first time *On the Buses* had been selected for the *All Star Comedy Carnival*. In 1969, during the first year of the series, a special Christmas short, filmed in black and white, was produced as part of the festive programming along with *The Dustbinmen* and various other choice favourites from the era. This earlier sketch has since, however, been totally wiped from archive and no copies, or even production notes, survive to shed light on what the plot may have been.

Having such a compilation of popular programmes from across the network was un-chartered television for the commercial ITV, and the *All Star Comedy Carnival* was one of the first occasions to feature mixed programming originating from independent networks. London Weekend Television, Thames Television and Granada Television; all who worked under their own identities as franchises of ITV, share their programming under one name ITV for this festive show.

Production

The sketch was filmed entirely on location at one of Eastern National's bus depots, most probably Wood Green. The appearance of many Eastern National buses in the background is proof that their services and vehicles, were used. Scenes are also shot in an Eastern National booking office, suggesting it was filmed at a bus station where public services terminated and commenced, rather than merely a bus depot where vehicles are kept.

As no part of the sketch was filmed in a television studio, the quality of footage is predictably poor, as it was filmed entirely on 16mm film cameras.

7

Reception

From the very first episode, the television critics saw weaknesses in *On the Buses* and were keen to shed an unfavourable light on the programme. "The critics never liked our comedies," explains Ronald Chesney, albeit rather glumly. "Critics don't like working class comedy, but that is all we ever did, that was the style of comedy we wrote. We didn't have a university education like John Cleese or the other Monty Pythons, so critics always looked down on our stuff. Even today, when the shows are repeated, all the TV magazines put 'rubbish, 1 star' in the reviews and it drives me mad."

With London Weekend Television's first sitcom, *Please Sir!,* attracting fairly positive press in 1968, it was important the station increased their repertoire of strong comedy. If both viewers and critics turned off, *On the Buses* would be an early casualty of the commissioning editor's experiment in comedy. Despite being panned by reviewers, viewers at home refused to change the channel, and the show became a fond family favourite.

"Audience matters most," explained the director Howard Ross. "Thankfully, people watched in their millions. We didn't have much pre-publicity before the show began, no more than the usual. We would have been in TV Times and a few interviews, so it was quite a surprise exactly how popular the show became. We had been fairly certain the show would work, but had no idea exactly how much, it was almost a follow on from *The Rag Trade*!"

"Luckily for us, LWT didn't take much notice of the critics," Ronald Chesney explained. "Their main priority was the viewing figures, and the first series went well."

The First Series of *On the Buses* ended on 11th April 1969, and based on viewing figures, a second series was commissioned midway through the transmission of the first, and began airing on television screens fifty days later, on 31st May 1969. "Frank Muir would have commissioned the second series as soon as we got the figures in for the first," Howard Ross confirms. "Cyril Bennett, programme controller, was chomping at the bit for a new series too. LWT had just started out, and it was vital we got the audience figures under our belt." *On the Buses* had made the vital acid test, and passed with flying colours. Although it could be suggested London Weekend Television were still desperate for more comedy on the station, and would happily have commissioned more of *On the Buses*, even if the ratings had been poor, with the ever present danger of a situation comedy vanishing after the first series, it was an admirable achievement for the show to be rated highly enough for a further run of episodes so soon after transmission of the first.

With the Second Series of *On the Buses* offering an opportunity of further exposure to the show, the audience figures increased, and by the end of Series Two were standing at a healthy 6.9 million households tuning in weekly, giving LWT enough confidence to wait six months before launching the third series on 2nd January 1970. It was the Third Series that permanently secured the fame of *On the Buses*. Transmitted for the first time in colour, and running for thirteen episodes, the same number as the previous two series combined, the Third Series lingered on the television long enough to be noticed by viewers and *On the Buses* became a regular choice for families across the nation. From here, so long as the show stayed funny and appealing, the future of *On the Buses* was assured.

By the time the Forth Series began, viewing figures had increased rapidly to 8.5 million households, making the show the third most-watched programme on commercial television. By this time, the success of the show had jumped from the small screen to reality and *On the Buses* was a regular feature in TV Times, as well as a comic strip version appearing in children's magazine *Look-In* from 1970.

The stars of the show were also much in demand, and off screen became hot choices for personal appearances at galas and as the ribbon-snipping celebrities at opening events and launches. Crowds swarmed to see Reg Varney opening John Walton Gentlemen's Tailors in the Chelmsford shopping precinct in 1970, and even the inaugural opening a housing estate in Braintree with the *On the Buses* cast present drew in the public.

With such widespread fame, it was fairly inevitable that occasionally, the public would get a little too close for comfort on the cast. "I felt like I had no privacy at all in *On the Buses*" Anna Karen recalled glumly. "A little boy knocked on my door at six in the morning - his dad was a milkman - and I answered it with an angry 'YES?!', and he asked if he could have my autograph, I said, 'Not at six in the morning you can't - come back later.' There was another time, which was perhaps the worst, when I was in this pub on New Year's Eve, this bloke came up to me and said, 'Here, you're the bird that never gets none,' and I said 'Yes?', and he said, 'I'm gonna do you a big favour' and I screamed 'No you're not!'. They did take liberties though. I've been called a silly cow in the streets once - although thankfully never a 'stupid great lump'."

In 1971, *On the Buses* had another chance to rapidly increase its audience, and with the release of the first film nationwide during the holiday season, the lure of being on the bus was too much to resist. The first film was a box-office sensation, and remains to this day Hammer Film's biggest money-spinner. "The films took more money than anything else," Ronald Chesney explained. "It was the most popular film that year, we even beat James Bond. It was the next year when we took *On the Buses* to America that we knew we had something - the show was a great success - and when you are big in America, you know you have made it. The series on LWT back home had fantastic ratings, we were at 18-20 million at our peak."

If critics were still debating the success of *On the Buses*, they wouldn't be much longer. The BBC decided to pitch their biggest audience-puller, *The Morecambe and Wise Show*, on a weekend slot to compete directly with ITV's bus-related sit-com. "We weren't happy being put up against *Morecambe and Wise*," Ronald Chesney recalls. "But we beat them! We got more viewers than the most popular programme on television!"

"This was the time when the BBC had monopoly on comedy," director Howard Ross explains. "But LWT came very close to toppling them and knocking them off their perch. We had *On the Buses, Please Sir!, The Fenn Street Gang, Doctor in the House*. We were putting out quality stuff."

But despite the outstanding popularity of *On the Buses,* critics will always remain, and *On the Buses* had its critics closer than it liked to think, as some of the crew who worked on the series declare they weren't the programme's biggest fans. Most surprisingly, Derrick Goodwin, the director of eighteen episodes, had negative opinions of the show. "I hated it!" Derrick explained. "I know not many people will say that, but I'm not going to lie, it just wasn't my cup of tea. I prefer the lighter type of entertainment like *Fawlty Towers, The Likely Lads*. I did a lot with Dick Clement and Ian LaFrenais, and I loved all their stuff, but I never really gelled with *On the Buses*. I was very new in television, and I did *On the Buses* for the experience more than anything, I had wanted to do a situation comedy for so long."

Another reason Derrick stayed was because he had an old

friend on the other side of the camera. "Michael Robbins kept me sane. He was a great friend, and I had known him for some time. I think he was the main reason I continued doing the show."

Other members of the production team had neutral thoughts towards the show. Sound supervisor Paul Faraday had mixed opinions. "I personally wasn't too keen on the show," he explained. "But it was another job, and we did what we were told."

Even today critics find fault with the show. Their main bore of contention were what they perceived as the apparent use of racism and sexism for comedic effect. "It was a different time," director Howard Ross explains. "You really need to remember it in context. Chalkie, for example, was never a problem then but that would be a huge issue today. Sexism too. I remember we wanted to get a low shot of this clippie walking up the stairs in a short skirt, which certainly wouldn't be allowed now. Also, Stan in general caused problems. Here is an old-ish man chasing young girls, that would be frowned on now. In reverse though, language has got much worse on television these days. I remember *Til Death Us Do Part* when Warren Mitchell was censored on how many times he said 'bloody' which is incredibly tame language by today's standards, the language is very strong, and it removes the aspect of family viewing."

To this day, *On the Buses* finds itself constantly repeated on television stations across the globe. "I know it's played an awful lot on ITV3," director Howard Ross explains. "Both through the day and in the middle of the night. The films are on very often too. It's seaside humour really, and that remains popular with British audiences. *On the Buses* goes in cycles, it dipped a bit in the Eighties and Nineties, and its interesting its back in vogue again now. They fall out of favour and come back, and its amazing sometimes exactly what comes back."

The writers of *On the Buses* are more than happy with the lasting legacy their brainchild has managed to sustain. "They showed *On the Buses* for an entire day a little while ago," Ronald Chesney recalled. "A full day of our sitcom on television, it's incredible, and this is over forty years since we wrote it. I'm biased of course, but I found it very funny. Looking at it now, I'm proud. I think we hit it just right."

"People still love the show," Anna Karen explains. "I was out shopping with Kate Williams and this lady came up to us and just said, 'Thanks for the laughs ladies.' There was another time I was walking down the seafront Rhyl where I was doing a pantomime. This man turned around to me and shouted, 'Olive!', and I looked around, and he said 'You're Grant's auntie in *Eastenders* now, but it will never be as good as *On the Buses*!'"

As Stephen Lewis aptly commented in a 1971 TV Times interview, "People like this show because it's about ordinary people, and it treats them with dignity and shows their self respect."

With such strong connection and bonds to its audience, it looks like *On the Buses* will be in vogue for many years to come.

8

Off to the Flicks

With immense television success, the chance of making a film version of *On the Buses* was too good a money-spinner to miss out on, and it eventually fell to production company Hammer, famous for their horror work, to put the buses on the big screen.

"Hammer needed to do a comedy film," Ronald Wolfe explained. "The first they did was *The Navy Lark*, but they were in financial trouble and needed a second." *On the Buses* had proven itself worthy of being the second Hammer Comedy production, after its phenomenal success on LWT.

It was also the saviour of the floundering Hammer Films, who were finding their original market, horror, increasingly difficult to compete in. Jimmy Carreras and Bernard Delfont (uncle of Michael Grade), both top people at Hammer Films, were keen to secure *On the Buses* as their next main comedy feature. Contractual issues made the plan move even faster. Instead of LWT holding the rights to any screen adaptations of *On the Buses*, they instead lay with writers Ronald Wolfe and Ronald Chesney. "I think us holding the rights was just luck," Chesney explained. "LWT had simply forgotten to ask for them when they drew up our contract!"

Hammer instantly had the green light to proceed to produce an *On the Buses* film, without having to seek permission from London Weekend to use their copyright, and instead simply approaching writers Wolfe and Chesney for clearance, which was happily issued. However, with LWT cut out of the big-screen adventures of *On the Buses*, funding for the film had to be sought elsewhere. "If I recall, they said they didn't think people would pay to see something at the cinema that they could see at home for free," Ronald Chesney remembered. "So instead we had to go to Bernie Delfont from Hammer Films. He, thankfully, loved *On the Buses,* so was able to fund the film, which came to just under £100,000."

Hammer production manager Christopher Neame also enjoyed the television programme, and was keen to make the first On the Buses film a success. "On the Buses was towards the end of my time with Hammer," Neame explained. "I joined them in 1956 with a Dracula film, and I was freelancing as production manager for the majority of their films, usually working with Roy Skeggs. *On the Buses,* I believe was the first comedy feature we did, and it was a pleasant change from horror. Hammer was fairly secure at that time. There was talk about it being in financial trouble, but Michael Carreras who had just taken over from his father in ownership of the company, put a good deal of money in it, and it was quite safe."

In July 1971, the first *On the Buses* film was released to incredible public reception, with total sales out-grossing both the James Bond flick *Diamonds Are Forever* and Michael Caine's *Get Carter* combined. With such an impressive first film, two subsequent *On the Buses* spin-offs, *Mutiny On the Buses* (1972) and *Holiday On the Buses* (1973), were also commissioned by Hammer.

On the Buses (1971)

Cast

Reg Varney - Stan Butler
Doris Hare - Stan's Mum
Michael Robbins - Arthur, his Brother-in-law
Anna Karen - Olive, his Sister
Stephen Lewis - Blakey, his Inspector
Bob Grant - Jack, his Conductor
Andrea Lawrence - Betty
Pat Ashton - Sally
Brian Oulton - Manager
Pamela Cundell - Ruby
Pat Coombs - Vera
Wendy Richard - Housewife
Peter Madden - Mr. Brooks
David Lodge - Busman
Brenda Gogan - Bridget
Caroline Dowdeswell - Sandra
Eunice Black - Ada
Claire Davenport - Peggy
Maggie McGrath - Gladys
Jeanne Varney - Mavis
Nosher Powell - Betty's Husband
Tex Fuller - Harry
Terry Duggan - Nobby
Anna Michaels - Eileen
Norman Mitchell - London Transport Official
Ivor Salter - 1st Policeman
George Roderick - 2nd Policeman
Gavin Campbell - Motor Cycle Cop
Hilda Barry - Old Woman
Jeanette Wild - Suzy
Moira Foot - Katy

Off to the Flicks

Reginald Peters - Medical Orderly

Main Crew
Production Supervisor - Roy Skeggs
Writers and Producers - Ronald Wolfe and Ronald Chesney
Director - Harry Booth
Production Supervisor - Christopher Neame
Director of Photography - Mark McDonald
Production Designer - Scott McGregor
Film Editor - Archie Ludski G.B.F.E

Made at EMI-MGM Elstree Studios
Hammer Films - 1971

The first *On the Buses* film, simply entitled *On the Buses*, was produced in 1971, capitalising on the success of the first four television series. Starring the full cast from the television series, and written again by Ronald Wolfe and Ronald Chesney, the film was shot at Elstree studios, Hertfordshire.

Small screen to big

With a lot riding on the success of the first *On the Buses* film, it was important to be certain that the transition from television to cinema would work, especially as Hammer was dabbling in new waters. "They had done comedy in the past, but not much," explained Hammer production manager Christopher Neame. "We took the change from horror to comedy all in our stride. It was progress but I was fairly sure that the programme would make a good film. Most people in those days had black and white television, so for an audience to get a chance to see their favourite show in the cinema, in colour, for an hour and a half, was a big draw. *On the Buses* had every chance of success, it was very popular and it would be hard for it not to do well. I think in the end it turned out to be the most successful film Hammer ever did."

Expanding the Plots

"With the films we could really open out," Ronald Chesney recalled. "We could do so much more with them compared to the television series. We could use the bus more, have more shots of it on the road, use the skidpan at Chiswick, and have many more stunts, like crashing into a telephone box."

The characters were also expanded and Olive became a mum. "Giving Olive a baby was just another way we could get some more laughs in the film," Chesney continued. "Babies in television studios are difficult but in a film they are a lot easier to work with. We could also get some more funny lines in. There is one scene where Olive is talking to Arthur and she tells him how the doctor said that now she is pregnant, he may have to give up some of his little pleasures. Arthur just blankly looks up and says, 'I'm not giving up my telly!'."

Moving to the big screen also prompted a change of heart with bus company London Transport, and for the first time, they gave their consent to writers, and now producers Ronald Wolfe and Ronald Chesney, to allow them to use some of their facilities. "London Transport had always declined in the past with the series, and we used Eastern National buses instead, but now that they could see the show was successful, they wanted to get in on the action, so in the film we had red buses instead of green. Red suited the show more, I feel."

London Transport allowed the use of their skidpan at Chiswick for the film, but still turned down the request to use their buses. Although the buses in the film were red, they were actually purchased by Hammer, and not loaned from London Transport specially for the film.

"London Transport just didn't want to do it," recalls Hammer production manager Christopher Neame. "They let us use the skidpan, and they even did a feature on the film for their staff magazine. But they didn't let us use their buses. I think it was a mistake, it could have got them some great publicity."

The red Bristol KSW5G buses used in the film were instead bought by Hammer, and sold on once they had finished with them, only to be bought back for use in the next film, *Mutiny On the Buses.* Ostensibly, a fleet of six vehicles were purchased for use in the film, with six different registration numbers identifiable from the movie, however, realistically, four buses, doubled up with dummy registration plates, would have been a more likely scenario.

The Bristol KSW5G bus was first produced by Bristol vehicles in 1952, and used in operation throughout the country. A couple of the buses used in the film had previously been on service with Eastern National in Basildon, coincidentally as a forerunner of the green Bristol Lodekka used in the television series of *On the Buses*, which took over services in the late 1960s.

A change in the buses also meant a change in uniforms, signage, and most importantly, the depot, all of which were different in the film to the television series. Location filming for the depot in the television series had been done at Wood Green, whereas the depot in the film was, rather unimaginatively, the entrance of studio five at Elstree film studios!

Plot

The main plot of the first *On the Buses* film centred on the introduction of female bus drivers. "With the women bus drivers introduced, the men are furious," Ronald Chesney explained. "We actually got that idea from a bus company in Nottingham. We read in the papers that the male drivers had gone on strike because of it, and thought that would work well as a storyline."

Blakey is the bright spark behind the introduction of female drivers but his plan soon backfires as Stan, Jack, and the other busmen put as many obstacles in the way as possible. Not only is Stan fearing he will have to answer to a female boss, he is more conscious about the loss of his overtime. Convinced the new drivers will reduce the extra shifts available to other drivers, and with Mum and the family back home worried about their finances, action has to be taken.

Butler's problems are worsened when he realises that Olive is expecting a baby. The shocked father, Arthur, puts the blame on the night the telly blew up, but another mouth to feed is one more reason for action back at the depot. Olive's attempts at bringing in a salary, by getting a job as the cook in the depot, backfire spectacularly, and she is replaced by a vending machine.

Jack hatches several cunning plans to dispose of the women drivers. Utilising the depot's workshop, he knocks up some canny "diversion" signs, putting them up around the town to force the women to drive in circles, arriving back at the depot minutes later. Another devious ploy is to put spiders in the cab of female driver, a plan that ends up with a bus crashing and Blakey having to answer to the police. Finally, perhaps the most underhand plot so far, Stan and Jack put diuretic tablets in the tea of the women drivers. After spending all day on the road, crouching behind bushes, and making frequent stops at public toilets, resulting in several complaints, one from a startled vicar, the women drivers' scheme is scrapped.

Stan is delighted to be without the women drivers, yet the management still have to make good their promise of employment to the girls. The only answer is to make them inspectors.

"I thought we made a very nice film," remarks Ronald Chesney. "There were a few great lines that are very memorable. My favourite is one that a little old lady says when the bus gets into the depot late. One of the women drivers had taken it on the motorway by mistake, and had to go twenty miles before she could turn around. The lady said 'I've been two and a half hours on this bus, and I only wanted to go to Tesco!'."

Off to the Flicks

Guest Stars

To broaden the plot, several guest stars expanded the cast of *On the Buses,* including Pat Ashton, Brian Oulton, Pat Coombes and Peter Madden. In her pre-*Are You Being Served?* days, actress Wendy Richard also appeared fleetingly in the film, as an annoyed housewife at the laundrette. Accompanying her in this scene was Reg Varney's daughter, Jeanne. "My appearance in the film was certainly my first work out of drama school," Jeanne explained. "The producer asked me to an audition and I was delighted to get the part. It was a very exciting day filming, I didn't know everything took so long in a film - it was nothing like the television series. I already knew the cast well, so it was great working with them again. I remember being a bit tentative when hitting Stephen Lewis with my handbag, but Dad said to me, 'Don't do it soft, really 'it 'im!' So I did. I think Stephen forgave me!"

Break a Leg

Moving to the big screen let *On the Buses* further expand with the stunts it could include.

"There was a scene we did at the London Transport skid-pan," recalled Ronald Chesney. "It involved Stan skidding the bus around a corner, and the Inspector falling off the back and skidding across the floor. Stephen didn't do this, so we had a stunt man in called Tex Fuller and he did that stunt. But when he flew off the back, he landed badly and he actually broke his elbow in the fall!"

Many of the cast did their own stunts. A particularly brave Anna Karen recalls, "The only time I used a stuntman was driving round the depot in the foam for the second film but all the other times it was me. When the side-car detaches taking

Olive to the hospital, that was me and doing that was scary as Michael couldn't even drive the motorbike. They usually towed us behind the filming car and he just steered!"

Producing the Movie

"The film all happened so quickly," explained production manager Christopher Neame. "We did it in just four weeks, which is exceptionally fast for a feature film. We were working so hard, and it just seemed to be in and out of the studios so quickly."

But sticking to a tight schedule was sure to have effects on the cast and crew, and this came to light when Christopher went home one night without realising that the next day of filming hadn't been arranged. "I went home and it dawned on me that I didn't have any locations arranged for the next day. We were filming at 8.30 in the morning, so I had to work very fast. I got up early, and quickly drove around the area of the studios to see if I could find anywhere suitable. I managed to find somewhere, drove back to the studio just in time, and just told everyone to follow my car. I just got away with it!"

Despite a few minor problems, the crew enjoyed their work with the film. "*On the Buses* was a lot of fun to produce," Neame continued. "The film was working well, the cast were professional. I don't recall too much about it but that is a good thing. Not having memories about it means it was a good film and went without a hitch. All the rushes worked, all the pro-

Spiders in the Cab

A memorable scene from the film involved house spiders being released into the cab of a woman bus driver (Pat Coombes). Whilst the driver is out on the road, the creatures begin to climb her legs. However, Pat Coombes wanted no part in the arachnid action and instead ordered a legs double to play out this scene.

duction went well. By and large I worked with Roy Skeggs as a fellow producer. He was a regular at Hammer but I was freelancing as his junior. *On the Buses* creators Ronald Wolfe and Ronald Chesney had a lot of influence in the film too, so we named them as producers on it." This action certainly pleased the writers. "Hammer let us be producers on the film, this meant we got two salaries!" Ronnie Chesney laughs.

Not on two salaries, however, was the cast of the show. "I got £75 a week for the film, and we worked on it for three weeks," Anna Karen recalls. "It was the highest grossing film ever made in Elstree, but we had hardly any money to work with. I stepped on a bit of broken glass and got a poisoned foot. It swelled up, so they got the film doctor over to have a look at it and he kept laughing saying it would need to be amputated, which practically made me have a nervous breakdown by the end of the week. Anyway, they eventually sent me home and called a taxi for me. They deducted the cost of the taxi from my wages, I was furious."

Ello Ello Ello

With a film crew running rampant through Hertfordshire, the making of *On the Buses* also attracted the attention of a certain local policeman. "Borehamwood is boring, but it suited the locations we needed so we filmed there an awful lot. This meant we had quite a run-in with the police," explains production manager Christopher Neame. "At first he was very suspicious, rather officious chap towards us, but in time, after I explained about the film, he became a good person to know. In *On the Buses*, he was the one who set up the scene with bus on the motorway, and in *Mutiny* he helped us too, he pulled a lot of stings for us - I'm fairly sure we even credited him in the film, his name was Les Humphries."

Unfortunately, no such person is credited in either *On the Buses* or *Mutiny On the Buses.* It is also apparent that Les has retired from the force. The police force contact supervisor at

Hertfordshire Constabulary explained, "There is no record of anybody by that name working for us at the present."

Back to Boreham

Location footage was filmed around the area of the studios in Elstree. In exterior scenes, the house used as the Butlers' house was situated at 2, Malden Road, Borehamwood, adjacent to where BBC Clarendon House, and the *Eastenders* set, now sits. "The houses all look the same in Borehamwood," explained Anna Karen, "so it took me a while to realise I was filming *EastEnders* next door to where I filmed *On the Buses* forty years earlier, it was weird in a way, but I guess it made a nice reunion!"

Introducing Little Arthur

Something that never happened in the television series was passing Olive with the gift of motherhood. "In the series we dropped the idea of having a child," Anna Karen explained. "They're too difficult to work with, I had a baby in *The Rag Trade*, and they cry when they want, they go to the toilet when they want - don't get me wrong I love kids to death but when you're in a sitcom and they cry over the laughter lines its not going to work."

Something, which came with motherhood, was a motherly craving for a certain food. In Olive's case, this was pickled onions but these weren't madly popular with the actress who had to consume them. "Don't mention pickled onions," Anna laughs. "I wasn't keen on them then, but I can't look at them now. I haven't eaten them since *On the Buses*!"

X-Rated light entertainment

A spoke in the wheel of any smooth running plan is inevitable and *On the Buses* proved no exception. In this instance, rather amusingly, the gentle family romp of a film had returned from the film censors' office with an adult rating.

"All films get sent off to the censors office," explained production manager Christopher Neame. "But for some reason *On the Buses* was given an adult rating, despite there being nothing of an adult nature in it."

With a national release of the movie set to coincide with the school holidays, an adult rating was a disaster for the production. The censor behind the rating was John Trevelyan, who was known by directors for his somewhat cautious nature when it came to categorising films. Prominent Hammers Films director, the late Roy Ward Baker, put down Trevelyan in his published memoirs as "a sinister mean hypocrite, treating his favourites with nauseating unctuousness." Trevelyan, who died in 1983, also had a firm dislike of films in the James Bond series, so much so that the 1995 released *Goldeneye* had its main villain named Alec Trevelyan allegedly in revenge from the producers. With a fiercely unpopular censor dishing out the ratings at the film board, the success of the first *On the Buses* feature film seemed to be doomed.

Thankfully, in 1971, John Trevelyan suffered a spell of illness, leading his temporary replacement as film censor. Taking over the reigns from him was Stephen Murphy, a friend of writers Wolfe and Chesney. Murphy was a self-declared fan of On the Buses, and with the film re-submitted to him for review, the certificate awarded was far more positive, and a general release of the always intentioned family film went ahead.

Music

With the move to the big screen came a need for a strong musical score to accompany the film. Instead of using library music like in the television series, Hammer commissioned composer Geoff Unwin with the job of coming up with a fresh sounding tune to open the picture with.

"Phillip Martell was head of music at Hammer," Geoff explained. "I had been working with EMI Records and doing some incidental music for television programmes, when I started doing some music for Hammer Horror. I did the music for one of their horror films, but the film was so awful it never got off the ground. Nevertheless, the soundtrack was released on a record by Columbia, so that's how I got started composing for Hammer."

After his initial stint with Hammer, on the dire horror film, Geoff was surprised to be asked back by the company. "I didn't expect it at all," he continued. "Hammer were in quite a bit of financial trouble, so I thought I'd seen the last of them. If I recall, a tobacco company called Carera had injected quite a lot of money in the them, and that's how they managed to stay afloat."

"I had never seen *On the Buses* when I was asked to do the music. I went home to my wife and said 'I've been asked to do this music', and she said we'd better put the TV on and watch and episode. We looked at it. Once. Then we watched it the following week."

After watching the programme, Geoff developed an idea of the style of music that the film version of *On the Buses* should include. "I got the idea it should be Londoners. Not so much cockneys, but London-type people. I thought they'd go down to the pub for their entertainment, so we had this Knees Up Mother Brown type thing. I also thought about the title *On the Buses*. It sounded like Omnibuses, and an omnibus is something that never ends, one part merges into another. So I wrote this music where one part merged into another, it could go on forever, but it fizzles out at the end, and trails away, like the bus leaving the depot."

With a few ideas jotted down, and a request of a "naughty, slightly risqué" set of lyrics from Phillip Martell, Geoff went to Abbey Road studios in London to produce a demo reel of the song. "I made the reel with quite a small orchestra, and then took it over to Hammer to see Phillip. They were filming *On the Buses* in the studio next door, so he went off for a minute and came back with Bob Grant and Stephen Lewis. I was standing there thinking 'I'm being auditioned by the Inspector now!', but they started tapping their feet and said they liked it."

After approval from musical producer and the cast of the film, Geoff was keen to make a final fully rendered version of the demo for use on the production. "Phillip said he'd use my track, but I reminded him it was just a demo reel. I wanted to do a full recording of it and render it with a full orchestra, but he wouldn't let me, because it would mean Hammer would have to pay for it, and they always tried to shave off costs from anywhere they could. I had set up the recording of the demo, and the demo itself was produced at the expense of Roger Ferris, who had the key to the studio door that day at Abbey Road, so Hammer got the song for free. Roger didn't get anything out of this set-up, so by way of thanks, I put his name on the credits of the song."

The *On the Buses* theme tune was very popular, and clearly had potential to rake in additional money if it was set on a general public release. With intentions to make a saleable record from his track, Geoff went to EMI. "EMI said they wanted the track, so then I phoned Reg Varney, who was an excellent pianist, and asked if he wanted to play the theme himself. Reg said that he knew the song backwards because it had been played everyday in the studio before filming to get the cast in the mood. He was happy to play a version of it himself for a release of the song, so long as his was on the B-side of the release of the main track, so that way he would get the same amount of royalties for his efforts."

Mutiny On the Buses (1972)

Cast
Reg Varney - Stan Butler
Doris Hare - Stan's Mum
Michael Robbins - Arthur, his Brother-in-law
Anna Karen - Olive, his Sister
Bob Grant - Jack, his Conductor
Stephen Lewis - The Inspector
Janet Mahoney - Suzy
Pat Ashton - Norah
Kevin Brennan - Mr. Jenkins
Bob Todd - New Inspector
David Lodge - Safari Guard
Tex Fuller - Harry
Caroline Dowdeswell - Sandra
Jan Rennison - Gloria
Damaris Hayman - Mrs. Jenkins
Juliet Duncan - Gladys
Michael Nightingale - Pilot
Roger Avon - Policeman (Safari Park)
Barry Linehan - Policeman (Mobile)
David Rowlands - Policeman (On Beat)
Nicolette Chaffey - Nurse
Dervis Ward - Angry Passenger
Wayne Westhorpe - Olive's Baby

Main Crew
Production Supervisor- Roy Skeggs
Writers and Producers - Ronald Wolfe and Ronald Chesney
Director - Harry Booth
Production Manager - Christopher Neame
Director of Photography - Mark McDonald B.S.C
Production Designer - Scott McGregor

Off to the Flicks

Film Editor - Archie Ludski G.B.F.E

Made at EMI-MGM Elstree and Windsor Safari Park
Hammer Films - 1972

The second film in the trio, *Mutiny On the Buses*, was released in June 1972, again starring the full television series cast, and directed by Harry Booth. The film was made in Elstree, and on location at the now defunct Windsor Safari Park.

Plot

Mutiny On the Buses sees the busmen reacting to the new short-tempered depot manager Mr Jenkins, who has been designated regional boss by the bus company head office. Jenkins is convinced that the slackness and bad attitude of the bus crews is avoidable, and sets about a complete overhaul of the archaic Town and District bus company, instantly causing ructions.

As well as his new boss, Stan has further problems. He has been going steady with Suzy, a clippie at the depot, and is adamant on settling down with her and getting married. Stan's mum is having none of it and is devastated to see her little chick planning to flee the nest. She is convinced the lack of her son's housekeeping income will put Butlers into the poor house. When Arthur gets made redundant from his job, Stan is forced to re-think his plan of a happy home away from his family.

Back at the depot, problems are still brewing with Mr Jenkins, including the failed plan of putting radio control in the bus cabs, and a disastrous emergency practice after a fire scare. To add to Stan's anguish, he has to teach Arthur how to drive a bus so he can apply as a driver at the depot.

Something positive does, however, come from Mr Jenkins

- his bright idea to run tour buses to Windsor Safari Park. Its a golden opportunity of over-time for Stan, and he is convinced that if he secures the driving position, he will get enough funds to start up a new life with Suzy. Alas, his antics at the depot have put him at the bottom of the potential drivers list, but when Arthur draws his attention to the fact Mr Jenkins has been philandering with a female clippie, he indulges in some blackmail. Stan gets the job on the safari park run, but as ever, plans never run smoothly.

The Second outing for On the Buses

Having seen how successful the first film was, the *On the Buses* cast were determined that instead of a flat, they should get a percentage of the overall revenue *Mutiny On the Buses* took.

"We demanded a percentage this time," Anna Karen explained. "But Hammer were not at all happy and did everything they could to avoid paying. They started saying how the film was rubbish, how the rest of the cast were all dropping out of it. They said Reg had dropped out and Bob had too. They were threatening to recast the film, they were so disparaging about it. My agent actually told me to drop out of it too, but I thought I'd hang on until the others had gone. Eventually, Hammer agreed to giving us a percentage, the day before we started filming, it was all left to the last minute. Hammer was in trouble financially, they wanted all the money they could get."

Foaming About

The script allowed many chances for stunts, one of which was particularly dangerous, and nearly caused Stephen Lewis to suffer a serious injury. "There's a scene in the bus garage with foam and I slipped in the foam and went into the pit under the bus," Lewis explained in a 2001 interview. "It was real foam we used to make it look good, and I went completely under it.

While I was down there waiting for the signal to come up, I realised suddenly, how dangerous it was because as I breathed in, the foam went into my throat and I suddenly rose up and started to choke. I tried to get out of the pit but it was all slippery, and I kept slipping back. It was one of the guys on the crew who realised how dangerous it might be and he started reaching down into the pit and grabbed me. I had to be given respiration. It was very, very dangerous. The scene itself looked very, very funny. The director said that it was well worthwhile.

There's also the scene with the lion in the bus, then the skid pan from *On the Buses*, lavatories blowing up - they're all very dangerous."

Other cast members revelled in messing about the foam. "That was so much fun," Anna Karen explained. "We were all told not to breathe in, and we were fairly scared at first, but once I was in there it was great, I didn't want to come up."

Monkey Business

"*Mutiny On the Buses* was done at Windsor Safari Park," Ronald Chesney explained. "We had a bigger budget for this film, so got some more stunts in. We were lucky enough to get the safari park for free, as the film got them a bit of publicity. In one scene there we had lions on the bus, and later there were these chimps that broke in. Reg Varney was wonderful in that scene, as he had to sit in the cab, with this monkey sitting on his lap with its bum in his face, he was marvellous!"

<u>Holiday On the Buses (1973)</u>

<u>Cast</u>
Reg Varney - Stan Butler
Stephen Lewis - Inspector Blake
Doris Hare - Mrs. Mabel Butler
Michael Robbins - Arthur
Anna Karen - Olive
Bob Grant - Jack
Wilfrid Brambell - Bert Thompson
Kate Williams - Nurse
Arthur Mullard - Wally Briggs
Queenie Watts - Mrs. Briggs
Henry McGee - Holiday Camp Manager
Adam Rhodes - Little Arthur
Michael Sheard - Depot Manager
Hal Dyer - Mrs. Coombs
Franco Derosa - Luigi
Gigi Gatti - Maria
Eunice Black - Mrs. Hudson
Maureen Sweene - Mavis
Sandra Bryant - Sandra
Carolae Donoghue - Doreen
Tara Lynn - Joyce
Alex Munro - Patient

<u>Main Crew</u>
Written and Produced by - Ronald Wolfe and Ronald Chesney
Directed by - Bryan Izzard
Production Supervisor - Roy Skeggs
Director of Photography - Brian Probyn B.S.C

Made at EMI-MGM Elstree Studios and on location in Wales
Hammer Films - 1973

Off to the Flicks

The third and final film, *Holiday On the Buses*, was produced in 1973. Michael Robbins and Reg Varney, who by this time had both left the television series, rejoined the cast one last time in Elstree and on location at Prestatyn Holiday Park in Wales. Wilfrid Bramwell, Henry McGee, Arthur Mullard, Queenie Watts and Maureen Sweeney all made guest appearances in the film.

Plot

After a spate of crashes and ensuing havoc at the bus depot, Stan, Jack and Blakey are promptly given redundancy. Thankfully, Stan and Jack manage to get a job at Pontin's holiday camp in Wales, working on the local tour bus to take the campers on excursions. Alas, they discover Blakey has been offered a post at the camp too - as security supervisor.

Nevertheless, Stan and Jack attempt to enjoy their time at the camp, and even invite the rest of the Butlers up for a holiday. With all members of the family at the same location, problems are inevitable. For a start, a motorbike incident causes the loss of luggage in a river, little Arthur ruins the chalet with an inky water pistol, and a cigarette chucked into a toilet containing watered down petrol causes numerous other lavatories to explode.

Butler and Harper also have women trouble. Jack has been holding secret rendezvous with Blakey's nurse girlfriend, and Stan is trying to get a quiet moment with a camper named Mavis away from her mother, to say the least, life at Pontin's is challenging. Then there is the small matter of Stan and Jack losing a double decker bus at sea...

I 'Ate You Butler! - The Making of On the Buses

Break a Leg

With the final film scripted, planned and ready to film, a problem struck the cast. Stephen Lewis broke his leg, and was in a plaster cast for the entire filming schedule. In a last minute change of the plot, Wolfe and Chesney had to adjust the script just days before filming commenced. "Stephen was doing DIY at home, and broke his leg," Ronald Chesney explained. "It was something we had to write in at the last minute, but we got away with it."

Going Pontinental

The majority of *Holiday On the Buses* was filmed on location at Pontin's Holiday Park at Prestatyn Sands, near Rhyl in North Wales. This meant all the cast had to stay on location, making *Holiday On the Buses* the most expensive film in the trilogy so far. "I wasn't doing *Holiday On the Buses*," explained Hammer producer Christopher Neame. "I was busy doing another film with Danny La Rue, but I can imagine that making the film would have been fairly expensive in comparison to the other two. We would have got Pontin's for free as they got the publicity, like Windsor did in Mutiny, but having all the cast and crew on location would have put the bill up."

Hammer films also paid for the cast's transport costs to Wales. "I got driven up there," Anna Karen recalls. However, Reg Varney, surprisingly, despite owning a Rolls Royce, let the train take the strain. "Reg got the train," Anna continued. "But you need to remember that by this time he'd had a massive heart attack, and that would have been a long drive for him."

The cast stayed locally for a several weeks, with the main characters remaining on location the longest and those with smaller parts nearby for a fortnight. "I believe I had two weeks in Wales," explained actress Carolae Donoghue. "I had my train fare paid, my hotel accommodation was accounted for. Actually, I thought I was very smart because I was being paid to do something I loved. I was cast in the film via my agent and I had seen some of the show on television. I thought it was good light-hearted humour with a simplistic trend that appealed to many ages. Prestatyn was a wonderfully healthy location and when not filming, I was able to walk to the beach and sit on the beautiful white sand dunes. I used to write poetry when sitting there, looking out to the ocean, probably dreaming of how famous I was going to be as a brilliant actress - ah, how times have changed!"

Working on location at a holiday park - In summer - did promote crowd control problems. "There were always crowds of people watching," Carolae continued. "Not only because they were intrigued with the filming, but because Reg and Bob were popular comedy figures at the time." Generally, the hordes of holidaymakers watching the production wasn't too much of an issue, as much of the film was made before the park opened for the season. When the public did arrive for their holidays, several were recruited as extras, which may have been a mistake. "I did a pantomime in Rhyl a few years ago," Anna Karen explained, "and half the audience had been extras in *Holiday On the Buses*. Although having holidaymakers in the film was a big mistake, they were, after all, on holiday, so they got bored and left." But there was fun to be had at the campers' expense. "There is a technical term in movie lighting called kill the baby, Anna continued. "It's when you tell the lighting man to stop the lights, you say kill the baby. Anyway, we were filming by the outside pool, and it was chaotic, and this baby was endlessly crying. Brian Izzard shouted 'kill the baby', and the look of horror on the mother's face was hilarious. We fell about laughing for ages!"

Working on location also led to the problem of finding places to film. The manager's house in *Holiday On the Buses*, was in fact shot outside of Pontin's, in the home of local councillor Tony Young and his wife Ann. Their hillside home was the perfect set, and was utilised for several days' worth of filming, with the crews arriving at 7am each day. "We knew the manager of Pontin's Ray Price," recalled Tony, "he put us in touch with the film crew. Director Brian Izzard and Michael Carreas from Hammer came up from London on the train to have a look around the house and decided it was the perfect place to film. All the cast turned up first thing in the morning, Reg Varney's double, his hairdresser, wardrobe mistress, producer, technicians, right down to the canteen staff. They built a camera platform in the front of our house to film the back door, which they replaced with their own door and cat flap so the Alsatian could squeeze through. The dog was brought up from Devon for that scene."

"After a day filming, they would send the films off on the train for processing," Tony explained. "They'd come back in the morning and we could go and see the rushes, which was exciting." Another exciting element was having the cast in their home everyday, but for one seasoned actor, Henry McGee, a mere hallway was a challenge. "Henry had to do a scene where he walked down the hall and unlocked a door. It took him 29 takes!" The film crew eventually ran out of time working on location, perhaps due to Henry's lack of unlocking ability, and the Youngs' property had to be photographed and recreated in Hammer studios back in London.

Filming at the holiday camp has undoubtedly left a long legacy at Pontin's. "We had a letter from someone who wanted to be put in the same chalet they used in the film," explained Dario, a chalet allocation manager at Pontins. "He gave us the number of the chalet but we couldn't find it and had to get out all the old charts for the camp. Unfortunately, during the years when we were owned by Scottish and Newcastle we had a big renovation and they knocked down 156 chalets, so there is a chance the ones in the film have been demolished."

There are, however, some things about Pontin's which thankfully remain. "The ballroom is still exactly the same," Dario continued, "Its' been painted black, but the layout is the same with the tiered seating, and also the chalets still have the original blue baths. But all this is going to change very soon as we are having a refit to bring the camp into the current century."

Guest Stars

The final *On the Buses* film featured many well-known guest stars, most notably Wilfrid Brambell of *Steptoe and Son* fame joined the cast to play Mum's admirer, Bert Thompson. Also appearing were Arthur Mullard and Queenie Watts, who played Wally and Lilian Briggs, the same characters they played in Wolfe and Chesney's sitcoms *Yus My Dear* and *Romany Jones*. Henry McGee, an actor becoming widely known for his work on the Benny Hill Show, played the holiday camp manager, and Maureen Sweeney, another export from Romany Jones, appeared as Mavis, Stan's love interest.

Kate Williams, by this time widely recognised for her role as Joan in *Love thy Neighbour* made an appearance in the film as the holiday camp nurse. "There was a tendency at the time to have people from other sitcoms play cameos in films," Kate explained. "So they got me from *Love thy Neighbour*, and Wilfrid Bramwell in from *Steptoe and Son*. I did a lot of work up in Wales. By this time I had been in two episodes of the television series, so I knew the cast very well, they were all very

Portrait of a Queenie

Playing Lilian Briggs was Queenie Watts, an actress who rose to fame in the early 1960s, developing her niche as the weathered-faced housewife-next-door. But there was more to Watts than met the eye, as off screen she was landlady at her own public house, the Ironbridge Tavern, set deep in the murky grey of London's Docklands. Together with her husband, Slim, Watts performed her own brand of blues, serenading patrons of her pub with the backing of an eight-piece band.

professional and charming, I wasn't made to feel an outsider at all. We were staying at a hotel which was attached to the holiday camp, I wasn't there as long as the others, I only had a few scenes so it was about a week, but they gave us a private dining room and we all went down for dinner every night together en masse. The cast all knew what they were doing, and it was fun to work on. Reg was a comic; Bob was an expert farceur; Michael was the odd one out as he was a classically trained actor and I did a musical with him after in the West End; but he had a great sense of comedy timing."

The gritty but intimate Michael Orrom directed 1964 documentary, Portrait of Queenie follows her life behind the bar and ambitions for her singing. Having only one dramatic role to her name by this time, in the landmark 1962 Joan Littlewood production *Sparrows Can't Sing* (incidentally written by Stephen Lewis and filmed in Queenie's pub) and long before her steady future in television seemed assured, the film shows Watts's journey from her poverty stricken roots on the Isle of Dogs to a steady career in drama. Despite being given the ticket to success, with the lure of an overseas record contract, Watts stayed fastened loyal to her roots and turned it down. "There's only one place for me - dear old London" comes the reply when a customer asks Queenie if she will ever move. Even when she answered the call to become an actress, appearing in iconic programmes like *Steptoe and Son* and leading the cast of the Wolfe and Chesney penned *Romany Jones* and *Yus My Dear*, Watts was always back at her pub afterwards and never lost touch with her London roots.

Queenie Watts lost a battle with cancer and died in January 1980, aged just 53. Her famous Ironbridge Tavern, 447 East India Dock Road, Millwall, which was a local haunt for dockers since 1852, called last orders ten years later after her death, closing in 1990. It was rebuilt to become The Inner London Hotel.

Off to the Flicks

Michael Robbins's wife, Hal Dyer, also appeared in *Holiday On the Buses,* playing the holiday camp manager's wife. "I didn't do much in *Holiday On the Buses,*" Dyer explained. "I didn't have scenes with Michael at all, he was down in London whilst I was recording my scenes in Wales. I was in Prestatyn for about a week. I just remember staying at this nice hotel with Henry McGee waiting for the call to film."

Playing Olive's son, little Arthur, was Adam Rhodes, a child actor who made *Holiday On the Buses* his film debut, prior to working on Reg Varney's variety show in 1974 and leaving the business. "Adam was fun to work with," Anna Karen recalls. "I haven't seen him for ages, but I met his parents again recently at a Water Rats convention. They said he is doing well."

Also in the film, be it only for a short while, were holiday-making crumpet Doreen and Joyce, played by Carolae Donoghue and Tara Lynn respectively. "I have some very good memories of the film," Carolae explained. "Both Bob and Reg were very professional. I was incredibly shy and it was my first (and last) bit part in a movie. They took the time to be courteous and encouraging which was very nice. It also rings a bell with me that Arthur Mullard was a very funny man when he wasn't filming."

The introduction of guest artistes was generally considered a positive choice by the cast. "The film certainly benefited from the guest cast," Kate Williams explained. "It couldn't not benefit, they were all strong comic performers and all great people. All of these people had started small and worked their way up, there was enough work for them to gain experience and practice. The industry is a very different creature now."

The Moon coming over the mountain

Olive's bikini turns out to be a few sizes too big for her and when she is kicked into the Pontin's swimming pool by her ever loving husband, Arthur, the bottoms are lost, leaving Olive vulnerable. A resulting scene, which is disgracefully cut from the majority of prime-time repeats of the film, sees Olive's posterior beaming through the swimming pool, allowing Blakey's memorable line "It's like the moon coming over the mountain." But Anna Karen was adamant that it wouldn't be her moon doing the shining. "That wasn't my bum," she laughs. "I wasn't going to do anything like that with the crew and cast I'd worked with for so long - so instead we got a double in. I don't remember who the double was, but I'd like to find out." The double, who alas remains unknown, was in fact brought up from London on the train especially for the scene!

Also losing articles of clothing was the holiday camp nurse, played by Kate Williams, who whilst seeing Blakey was having a sneaky bit on the side with Jack. "I have not gone over this area since!" Kate points out. "But there was a scene where I had to strip down to bra and knickers. I wasn't desperately happy about it, but it was all postcard humour. It wasn't taken seriously."

Still at it...On the Buses

In early 1973, a little known plan was on the cards. The project, provisionally entitled *Still at it...On the Buses*, was supposed to be the planned fourth film in the *On the Buses* spin-off series.

The film was due to be produced immediately after the release of *Holiday On the Buses*, but no other details of the venture survive.

The plan clearly never made it out of the Hammer offices, as series creators Ronald Wolfe and Ronald Chesney deny all knowledge of the picture. "There was never going to be a fourth film," they explained.

Hammer production manager Christopher Neame hadn't heard of this plan either. "I don't know anything about that idea," he explained. "It could have worked quite well, as the first three were successful, but all ideas dry out - I don't think there is four films worth of comedy in a plot about bus drivers."

Although the possibility of a fourth instalment of the *On the Buses* film series sounds tantalising to fans, unfortunately the idea was no more than speculation. Looking at early production paperwork from *Holiday On the Buses,* it is evident that *Still at it... On the Buses* was in fact a provisional title for the third film, *Holiday On the Buses,* and no fourth movie was ever planned.

9

Gone Stateside

Lotsa Luck

Several British comedy classics were remade in the States during the 1970s and it was clear British comedy had great appeal to a transatlantic audience. Having already come up with *Sanford and Son,* in answer to Galton and Simpson's *Steptoe*, and *Thicker than Water,* snatching the idea from Hylda Baker's iconic *Nearest and Dearest*, TV network NBC were keen to bag *On the Buses* to add to their portfolio of exported humour. The idea developed into *Lotsa Luck.*

It was the renowned director and actor Carl Reiner who had the bright idea, together with Bill Persky and Sam Denoff. "I think also Michael Grade had influence in getting the series done over there," recalled Ronald Wolfe. "There was another television producer called Don Taffner [who produced the *Man About the House* remake *Three's Company*] but he didn't like us all that much."

But transporting this particular British sitcom to overseas audiences proved problematic, mainly surrounding the situation it was based on. "The plot didn't work with buses at all," Ronald Chesney explained. "In America they couldn't really relate to it because they don't really take buses, they take taxis. So Lotsa Luck was based solely on the domestic life of the series, with Stan's family at home. They also changed his job, he wasn't a driver. He worked at the lost and found department of the bus company."

The characters names also changed, although forenames reflected the British television series, the American counterparts' surnames had to be altered. Dom DeLuise played Stan Belmont and Kathleen Freeman, who played Iris (Mum) Belmont, joined him. Olive Swann was played by Beverly Sanders, with her husband, Arthur, portrayed by Wynne Irwin. Stan's friend at the depot, the dubiously named Bummy Pfitzer, was played by Jack Knight.

Many of the original plots were used to develop the scripts for Lotsa Luck, but not all of these worked in America. "I remember they remade the toilet episode, where Stan takes the cistern home on the bus," Ronald Chesney recalls. "The critics were astonished, and they wrote fierce reviews of it. They were horrified that they dared to show a toilet on the television, they were very prudish." For *On the Buses* fans, watching *Lotsa Luck* conjures many cases of deja vu as the majority of British episodes were remodelled. The episode 'Olive's Present' sees the family all go down with flu, 'The Bare Facts' sees Stan and Olive suspecting Arthur of having an affair; 'You Oughta Be In Pictures' has Stan applying to be the face of the company's advertising posters, and 'Mom's Secret' sees Iris go on a date.

With its similarity to *On the Buses*, and in spite of a few initial teething troubles with the show, *Lotsa Luck* was a huge success. "It went exceptionally well," Ronald Chesney continued. "There were phone calls and telegrams going back and forth between the studios and the William Morris agency, who represented us. They thought so much of it, they put it up against American football in the ratings."

That decision was the beginning of the end for *Lotsa Luck*, and viewers deserted the show in favour of watching sport.

"You don't get a second chance in the States, so that was it for *Lotsa Luck.*"

However, it may be construed as a good thing that the show came to an end, as it wasn't particularly popular back home with *On the Buses* creators, Ronald Wolfe and Ronald Chesney. "We didn't think much of the American version, but we went along with it," they explained. "We didn't really have a choice." Looking back on the show, one plot flaw, which could have made a difference to the show, is clear. "We should have made the inspector black." Chesney remarked. "It was at a time when American television was starting to offer more chances to black actors. It could have related to the audience so much more, it would have made all the difference."

Gone Stateside

On the Buses - A New Life

Having built up an incredible following overseas, *On the Buses* soon became adapted for the stage abroad. This version would be played in Canada in 1986, in Vancouver, and return the next year for a stint in Toronto.

A Canadian production team approached actress Kate Williams, who had in the past appeared in *Holiday On the Buses* and two episodes of the television series, with their sights on getting *On the Buses* across the Atlantic. "The motivating force being the show was a Canadian called Bill Simpson," Kate explained. "*On the Buses* had aired on Canadian TV and become exceptionally popular over there, and he thought it was perfect for an adaptation on the stage. He thought I would have the connections to make it work. Together we formed a production company called Angel Productions." Angel comprised Kate Williams, in creative, executive producer Bill Simpson, and general manager Terry Dickson, who had previously worked as stage manager on the British theatre adaptation of popular sitcom *George and Mildred* in 1979.

Having been told the plan, Kate got in contact with writers Ronald Wolfe and Ronald Chesney with a view to them penning the scripts for the show, and they met the idea with enthusiasm. "I managed to get in touch with them both and ask them about the show," Kate continued. "They were happy to help, devised a storyline and produced the scripts." Wolfe and Chesney recall receiving the invitation. "We were told there was a Canadian production company wanting to make a stage show of *On the Buses*, and we were asked about doing the scripts for it," Chesney recalled. "But we were only asked to write in Olive, Arthur and Mum, they didn't want the others for some reason."

Because of international Equity rulings, only three British actors could make the trip to Canada. "That was the first rule we were told," Kate Williams explained. "We could only have three British actors, and the rest had to be Canadian, otherwise the Canadian actor's union wouldn't allow us to do it. This was the problem at the time, I remember the *Love thy Neighbour* team went to Australia but had to leave me behind as they could only take three of us. Having just three of the characters from *On the Buses* also meant we had to think of a situation for them to explain why the others were missing. We all decided on a rough plot that Arthur, Mum and Olive had tried to emigrate to Canada, and they ended up in a rather seedy boarding house, which we filled with Canadian actors, and that got us round the Equity problem." Those actors included Ann Warn Pegg, Gary Chalk, Lynda Boyd, Ron Halder and Duncan Fraser.

With the emigration to Canada plot the general base of the play, the production was christened as *On the Buses - A New Life*. "The plot was very sketchy," Kate Williams recalled. "It was a farce, and there wasn't too much faith put in to how realistic the show was. Olive, Arthur and Mum would never be able to move to another country. It's just not the sort of thing they would be capable of, they couldn't board a plane and go - It just wasn't their character but we got round it. The main thing we needed was to have the three of them in the boarding house, where most of the action took place. It was quite a seedy setting. There were a few ladies of the night around the place, and, of course, Arthur is totally disgusted by it, and Olive, in her innocence, finds it all quite fun."

The programme for *On the Buses - A New Life* explains how the show is set in a hotel on Granville Street, Vancouver, which in reality is the main tourist street in the city, with the majority of the city's hotels. "If I recall the plot, we all ended up having to work in this hotel to make money," explained Anna Karen, who reprised her character of Olive in the production. "They wanted the premise of me, mum and Arthur moving to Canada. Arthur sells the return plane tickets or something, so we get stuck there. I remember we did the first year in Vancouver, and I went back the second year to Toronto, it was very popular."

But the return to Canada the second year caused problems for the cast, namely Doris Hare, who was busy with other projects. "They had to recast the show for Toronto," recalls Michael Robbins's widow Hal Dyer. "Doris was busy, so instead they got Claire Kelly in the part. I went with Michael to Vancouver to see the show and it was very successful and went rather well. The Canadians were mad about *On the Buses*. If I recall, they also did a tour of the show in Australia and New Zealand a few years later, the overseas appeal of the programme was amazing."

But despite clawing in the dollars across the Atlantic, there was a perfect opportunity for a British tour of an *On the Buses* stage show that was left neglected. "I don't know why we never did a British tour of *On the Buses*," explains Anna Karen. "It would have worked very well on home territory. The closest it came to was a farce I did in Great Yarmouth with Bob Grant and Stephen Lewis called *Stop it Nurse*, but I do feel a British tour of *On the Buses* would have gone down a storm."

Hal Dyer concurs. "There was the opportunity," she says. "But it was never taken, which is a shame, it could have been a great show."

Directing On the Buses - A New Life

The driving creative force behind getting the production on stage was Canadian director Mario Crudio. "I directed both the Vancouver and Toronto plays," Mario recalled. "It became a very successful show and I found a few days ago, quite by accident, a review of the show at the time - the critics were very favourable towards it."

10

Decline and End

All good things come to an end, but the end to *On the Buses* was a gradual one. The general decline of the programme started more than a year before the transmission of the last episode. It commenced in the Fifth Series, when creators, and up to then, writers, Ronald Wolfe and Ronald Chesney, handed the reigns of the show over to other wordsmiths.

"We needed to do other things," Wolfe explained. "We had to do the *On the Buses* film, the scripts for them, and get all that sorted, and then there was little time left to write the series for LWT." As well as the films, an American version of *On the Buses*, entitled Lotsa Luck, was also being created, and required Wolfe and Chesney to head to the States to assist with the spin-off.

At first, the show's stars Bob Grant and Stephen Lewis collaborated on several scripts in the Fifth Series of the programme. Having already worked together on many occasions, stemming from a strong working relationship at Joan Littlewood's Theatre Workshop at Stratford East, the duo were responsible for scripting twelve episodes over the final three series. Derrick Goodwin directed most episodes. "I remember doing Bob and Stephen's scripts, as well as Ronnie Wolfe and Ronnie Chesney's," Derrick explained. "It was always difficult

Decline and End

taking over something that you hadn't started and I think they did a very good job. The rest of the cast didn't seem to react against them in any different way, and I don't think any judgement was held against them."

Bob Grant and Stephen Lewis were always conscious of not over-inflating their parts as they took over writing the show. "The hardest part is not writing our own parts up too much," Bob explained to *TV Times* in 1971. "We've been working on the show for three years now, so it isn't difficult for us. We know the characters, and we know what situations we have used before. Whilst we attempt to keep our own parts small, it's also important for us not to write our own parts down, that's the only real difficulty."

Jonathan Lynn and George Layton were another writing duo who penned episodes, and contributed the majority of episodes featured in Series Six. "I think the invitation for us to write some episodes came from Ronnie Wolfe and Ronnie Chesney," recalled Lynn. "I had hardly ever seen *On the Buses* before, and we found it very difficult to write in the style of Wolfe and Chesney. After all, we had not created this show but the cast were rather nice about it, and seemed perfectly friendly. LWT seemed to regard us both as hot, new comedy writers, because of our work with *Doctor in Charge*. There is always a dearth of such people. We seemed the right choice for *On the Buses,* we could get the laughs and because we were fairly new, we didn't have any commitments. Our first show was very well received by fans, which was surprising. We even had a nice review in the The Times. I always remember Wolfe and Chesney to be so kind and supportive, and we struggled to emulate their success."

The loss of the original writers was the first nail in the coffin for *On the Buses*. Despite the new episodes getting good press reviews, the cast and the creators weren't desperately keen on the direction the show was going in. "We weren't too happy with leaving the show," Ronald Chesney explained. "The new writers were good, but I think the style of scripts were too different to our own and the audience seemed to notice."

The cast weren't exactly enamoured by the new script writers either, mainly with the jobbing writers who penned individual episodes in the seventh series. "We had many writers brought in to do the shows after Wolfe and Chesney left," Anna Karen explains. "Bob and Stephen were good, as were Jonathan Lynn and George Layton, but some of the others were awful. I think there was one episode I did with Yootha Joyce called 'The Allowance' and that was very weak."

Losing the Cast

As well as missing the original writers, the stars of the show were also leaving. The first to go was Michael Robbins, who, despite popular belief, did not flee because he felt the show was progressing in the wrong direction but took up an attractive theatre offer in London's West End.

"Michael was offered a part in *Time and Time Again* with Tom Courtenay," his widow Hal Dyer explained. "Theatre was always his first love, and this part was excellent, a really funny character in a comedy. He was thrilled to appear in it. When he joined the cast, nobody knew how long the production would go on. It could have gone on forever but it was decided to bring it to an end fairly soon. By this time, it was too late for Michael to go back to *On the Buses* on LWT, but he did return for the film *Holiday On the Buses*. We both knew director Brian Izzard, and he thought it would be a nice tribute for Michael to go back with the rest of the old gang one last time."

Robbins left before the start of Series Seven, and he missed the final thirteen episodes. His departure was explained in a storyline that saw him finally divorce Olive. The trauma left her in a fragile mental state for the majority of the final season. "We weren't in the UK when Michael left," explained Ronald Wolfe. "But he was a very good actor, and always in demand. He was typecast towards the end, and everyone knew him as

Decline and End

Arthur."

But one more cast member was still to hang up his bus driver's hat for the last time. Most surprisingly, Reg Varney, left mid-way through the Seventh Series. His departure was explained in the series by Stan moving to the Midlands to work in a car factory.

Varney, who had been with the show for an incredible sixty-eight episodes was sad to leave, but felt that the programme was nearing its natural end. "Dad decided the show had had a good enough run by the time he left it," explained Reg's daughter, Jeanne. "Perhaps the new writers were not so good, but I think he just didn't want On the Buses to be remembered as being repetitive and less funny as it surely would have been. Shows have a natural limit and *On the Buses* had to come to that limit." Reg did, however, return along with Michael Robbins, to appear in *Holiday On the Buses* in 1973. "That film had a very funny script," Jeanne continued. "It also made a nice goodbye to the series."

With two of the most popular characters now missing from *On the Buses*, the last episodes of the sitcom struggled by but still managed to tickle the funny bone. Actor Albert Moses, who appeared in 'Friends in High Places', the penultimate episode of the last series, says that the loss of cast members had little effect on the programme. "The atmosphere of the programme was not affected," Albert explained. "One gets used to working with different actors all the time, and we have to learn to fit in with the changes. The newcomers are always nice to the previous cast, and get along very well. It didn't look like the show was affected. Change of cast is so common that you simply take it for granted and carry on regardless."

At the end of the Seventh Series, the cast of *On the Buses*, together with the writers, decided to call it a day. "We knew before we started the seventh series, that it would be our last," recalled Anna Karen. "We knew Reg was leaving and I had to divorce Arthur to cover his absence. We decided to call it a day there and go out on a high. I don't think the final few episodes where it was just four of us made us more popular in any way. We all got a fair crack of the whip - I always got a lot of lines, and they were good lines."

London Weekend Television were reluctant to accept their most popular programme was drawing to a close but with regret, the depot doors were closed for the last time, some seventy-three episodes after the pilot, and an astonishing five years since the Luxton and District bus company started business. Truly, this was the end of an era.

But the end to *On the Buses* could have been avoided, and writers Ronald Wolfe and Ronald Chesney feel sure that their initial absence from the series was the first catalyst that finished the show off. "If we had have continued writing, then we would have kept going," Insisted Ronald Wolfe. "I know that we would have done at least one more series, so we would have had eight in total, but after that, there would have been a chance of ideas running out, and we probably would have stopped then, when we were all still at the top of our game."

11

Senior El Blakey

"LWT had a few rough patches where they needed more comedy," explained Ronald Wolfe. "In the mid-1970s we remade a lot of our older programmes for them, and also came up with a new one using Stephen Lewis again - Blakey had been a hit in *On the Buses* and we tried to find something that suited him."

Together, Ronald Wolfe and Ronald Chesney eventually came up with *Don't Drink the Water,* a show starring Stephen Lewis reprising his character of Blakey, joined by Pat Coombes, who played his sister. "We were originally going to use Thora Hird in this part," Ronald Chesney recalled. "She had been in Meet the Wife and was very good, but we eventually got Pat Coombs, who had appeared in The Rag Trade."

Don't Drink the Water was a loose spin-off from *On the Buses*, and featured Blakey upping sticks from the depot in Luxton and moving to Spain with his sister. Inevitably problems occured including the state of the apartment they foolishly purchased without a viewing, a language barrier, and a block of flats being built to obstruct the "fine views of the sea", means Blakey's retirement seemed doomed to failure. Boldly utilising every available stereotype of Englishmen having nasty experiences abroad, such as brown water in the plumbing, corrupt policemen, and badly built housing, *Don't Drink the Water* was supposed to burst onto the television with a fanfare and capture audiences nationwide, even being promoted with a front cover feature on the TV Times. The plan failed.

Ingenious plots for episodes, including 'The Smell' - which revolves around a pong from the drains, and 'What, No Telly?', a self explanatory title which could almost stem from a Chad sketch, viewers could be forgiven for thinking the show was weak in ideas and humour.

Don't Drink the Water, which was broadcast for two series between 1974 and 1975, just one year after the final nail had been hammered in the coffin of *On the Buses*, tried its utmost to rekindle the chemistry of it's ratings-winning predecessor.

Alas, the general consensus among viewers showed that the programme flopped, and has since been ranked within the top five of a poll of Britain's worst sitcoms - a fact that the writers know only too well. "It wasn't a great success," they explained. "It's best forgotten really - with *On the Buses*, every member of the cast were wonderful. With other sitcoms we didn't have the same cast, and it didn't work well at all."

12

Back to Rags

As well as reusing Stephen Lewis, writers Ronald Wolfe and Ronald Chesney also called upon Anna Karen to reprise her character, Olive, in the 1976 remake of *The Rag Trade*. Whereas *Don't Drink the Water* was a spin-off from *On the Buses,* the revival of *The Rag Trade* was heralded as a completely different show with no links to *On the Buses* at all, so to call upon a well-established character from a different programme to play the same part in something else was an unusual tactic. In fact this interesting technique was one of the only two examples in British comedy, the only other occasion being Arthur Mullard and Queenie Watts in *Holiday On the Buses,* playing the same parts as they did in LWT sitcom *Romany Jones.*

Anna Karen recalls the day she was recast as Olive. "Ronald Wolfe phoned me up and asked me to do *The Rag Trade*," she recalls. "It was fun to be Olive again, but it did surprise me how long in between series it was. There had been five years since *On the Buses* ended, but people still recognised me as Olive, and *On the Buses* hadn't been repeated in between."

The Rag Trade character was only loosely based on the original *On the Buses* Olive and some continuity mistakes between series are evident. "In *On the Buses,* I divorced Arthur," Anna

Karen explains. "Yet in *The Rag Trade*, we're married again, and I even have a baby." But Karen goes on to divulge how continuity was never top of the to-do list. "It's only little minor details, but people still point that mistake out to me. I don't think continuity is too important though, I do an episode of *EastEnders* and I recognise the fact that I've got the same bit of dialogue I had four weeks ago, but the writers don't worry about it."

Aside from Stephen Lewis and Anna Karen, the other members of the cast weren't reused in other sitcoms reprising their old characters. "I remember both *The Rag Trade* and *Don't Drink the Water*," exlpained Michael Robbins's widow, Hal Dyer. "Michael never got a spin-off.. Work was always lean for him. He did get a Variety Club Award though and appeared on *This is Your Life* for Reg and Doris."

The year of 1976 also saw the rebirth of another Wolfe and Chesney sitcom. This time it was *Yus, My Dear*, which was an adaptation of the previous hit *Romany Jones*. Two series of this new programme were made, starring the regular duo of Arthur Mullard and Queenie Watts, as Wally and Lil Briggs, joined by comedian Mike Reid who played loitering oik Benny.

The show wasn't a major hit and tends to centre around the recurring theme of Wally annoying Lil and trying to introduce the catchphrase "I ain't fick" whenever his intelligence is questioned. Even the writers don't look back fondly on the show. "*Yus, My Dear* was awful," Ronald Wolfe's wife, Rose recalls. "It was the worst series the Ronnies ever wrote, it was shocking. It was not worthy of them at all. It just didn't work. Arthur Mullard was a character, not an actor. He had been a boxer I think. At that time, LWT was desperate and they were willing to grab anything. *Romany Jones, Yus, my Dear* and *Don't Drink the Water* were all weak."

One success that did seep from the pens of Ronald Wolfe and Ronald Chesney was *Take a Letter Mr Jones*, a sitcom made for Southern Television in 1981, and starring John Inman and Rula Lenska. "That series was great," continued Rose

Wolfe. "John Inman said it was one of the funniest things he had been in." But unfortunately, only six episodes were ever made. "Southern TV came to the end of its franchise." Rose explained. "The new company wanted to start afresh and we didn't do any more. I think though, if it had of gone further, it would have been a great hit."

Take a Letter Mr Jones was one of the last sitcoms Wolfe and Chesney worked on, aside from scripting a couple of episodes of Jeremy Lloyd and David Croft's wartime farce *'Allo 'Allo* in 1982.

13

Back On the Buses

In 1990, viewers of *Wogan* were astonished when the full cast of *On the Buses* assembled on stage to discuss plans for a revival series. At first, Reg Varney walked over to Terry Wogan's sofa, and after a chat about his early life and career, the rest of the cast joined him to discuss the prospects of *Back On the Buses*. "The old gang are still incredibly popular," explained Varney, gaining huge cheers for the audience. To all intents and purposes, a revival of *On the Buses* seemed to be definitely on the cards.

The idea sounded tantalising to fans but it soon became apparent that the proposed *Back On the Buses* would not materialise.

"I got the feeling that working class comedy was starting to become quite a has-been," explained Rose Wolfe. "Television wanted more sophisticated stuff. The Ronnies wrote storylines for the new *On the Buses* revival, but it didn't go very far. I can't recall whether it had even been commissioned."

The plot of the show was very vague. "If I recall, Stan starts a coach hire company" explained Anna Karen. "He works there, and hires Jack as a conductor, and Olive's son becomes a driver there too. I think Blakey works at the licensing department for the bus company, and is against the idea, so tries to stop it going ahead."

Despite the sketchy ideas, *Back On the Buses* had caught the interest of one television station, but unfortunately the company in question hit the rocks soon after the idea was developed, putting paid to any further progress to revive *On the Buses*. It was, however, too late to stop the cast appearing on *Wogan* to tell excited audiences the show was making a comeback. "We all got back together for Wogan," Anna Karen remembers. "But from the start, the idea was very poorly thought out. Only a few of us had actually been told about. I was phoned, and I believe they called Stephen and Reg, but the others had no idea about the revival - they only found out on the day we went to record the interview with Terry Wogan."

For some inexplicable reason, the producers didn't bother to alert Bob Grant, Michael Robbins or Doris Hare that *On the Buses* was destined to make a comeback It was a decision that was very upsetting for at least one member of the cast. "Michael had to ask me what was going on, but he dealt with the news quite well, as did Doris, but Bob was so very upset that he hadn't been told," Anna continued. "He was deeply shocked, I hadn't seen him that upset before. And once that show had been recorded, none of us ever heard from Bob again." Despite repeated attempts to telephone and write to him, Grant cut off all contact with the rest of the cast, the team he had worked with professionally for five years and been friends with socially for more than twenty. "We have no idea where he went or what happened to him," explained Anna. "He didn't even contact Stephen, and they had known each other for many years, written together, and worked together many times."

Back On the Buses eventually fell through, the main reason being the collapse of the production company behind it. "We would have tried to get the idea taken on by someone else, but television was undergoing many changes," explained writer Ronald Chesney. "Most of the people we knew had left the business, and there were a lot of younger executives creeping in. Anything that harkened back to an old idea, no matter how successful the first one was, was considered out of date. We even tried to get *The Rag Trade* back for a third time, but nobody wanted to know".

"I knew no more of a whisper about *Back On the Buses*," explained director Howard Ross. "I'm not sure it would have worked really, the BBC did an *Are You Being Served?* spin-off and people tend to associate old characters with old shows, so using them again doesn't always work. The BBC also brought back *Doctor in the House*, but it was a flop. Too much time had passed really, viewers do like the old but they also like the new."

The chances of an *On the Buses* revival were now very slim, but worse news was in store for the team. Michael Robbins, who played Arthur, was in the final stages of cancer, and finally succumbed to the disease in December 1992. "Lots of people think it was Michael's death with halted *Back On the Buses*," explained his widow, Hal Dyer. "But this isn't the case. He did have to limit his workload but he was always in demand. At one point he was even lined up to take over from Sid James in the *Carry On* series, but that never happened."

14

Cast Appendix

<u>Reg Varney</u>

Reginald Alfred Varney was born on 11 July 1916 in Canning Town, London. The son of a rubber factory worker in Silvertown, and one of five children, he attended Star Lane Primary School, Canning Town.

A keen piano player from an early age, it was his impressive instrumental skills and general showmanship that secured Reg his first public performances. After leaving school at fourteen, Varney started work as a messenger boy at the Regent Palace Hotel in London, prior to obtaining a paid position as a pianist at the Plumstead Radical Club in Woolwich.

During the Second World War, Varney served with the Royal Engineers in the Far East, progressing his entertainment repertoire with gang shows and army concerts. This fuelled Varney's ambition to perform, and following demobilisation he returned to England, appearing in the revue *Gaytime*, alongside another future comic Benny Hill.

A tour of variety halls led Reg to television, and his first major role, as cutter Reg Turner in *The Rag Trade*, in 1961. Further television followed, and after a brief hiatus due to a heart attack, Varney added to his success in the 1967 sitcom *Beggar My Neighbour*. A rise in public fame led him to becoming the celebrity of choice to open the world's first automated telling machine or cashpoint at Barclays Bank, Enfield, on 27 June 1967. Cast in *On the Buses* the next year catapulted Varney to stardom, and he stayed with the series for sixty-eight episodes, when he decided to hang up his bus driver's cap and overcoat and focus on his variety work. Varney also returned to classical acting, to appear in a remake of his 1969 television hit play *The Best Pair of Legs in the Business.*

Still a popular celebrity, Reg also put in appearances at numerous charity events and galas, notably the Jersey Battle of the Flowers competition. "I didn't go to the Battle of the Flowers," explained Reg Varney's daughter, Jeanne. "But I went to a lot of the award dinners, mainly because my mum didn't like them, but I did. Dad was always really proud of the success and the awards, but mainly I think he enjoyed the fact that ordinary people, like the Stans and Jacks, really liked the series and enjoyed his work. Dad had come from that kind of family himself growing up."

In 1975, Reg began concentrating on his own brainchild, a sitcom centring around the life of a fish porter at Billingsgate Market, entitled *Down the Gate*, however the series wasn't a major hit and viewers found it difficult to think of Reg in a new non-bus related, role. "I think there was always a chance of typecasting," Jeanne continued. "Stan had so much of dad in him that it was inevitable. I think dad would have loved to do straight acting, which he was very good at, but he never got the chance. He did, however, do a lot of work in Australia, which he loved, until he got a heart problem and retired."

Varney suffered his second major heart attack in 1981 and chose to take life at a slower pace afterwards. He returned once more to Australia, a place where he was still very much a celebrity, having co-starred with Billy Raymond in the Channel O production of *Rose and Crown* which ran for thirteen episodes back in 1969, and he toured with his cabaret act to packed theatres across the country. In 1988, he returned once more to resume his role as Stan in an Australian *On the Buses* stage play.

Soon after his return to England, Reg felt it was time to leave the public spotlight and he retired to his home in Budleigh Salterton, Devon. "He always said he was never stagestruck," Jeanne Varney explained. "He enjoyed his career and his retirement in Devon with my mum."

Varney took time from his absence in television to write his autobiography, *The Little Clown*, although a second promised volume never appeared. The first one stopped before his time at the Luxton and District Bus Company. He dedicated his time to piano playing and painting. Among his many talents, Reg was a skilled artist.

In 2002, Varney's wife, Lillian, died at a local nursing home. Six years later, on 16 November 2008, Reg himself died in the same nursing home following admittance for chest pains. He was cremated and his ashes reunited with his wife in the same unmarked burial plot in the grounds of St. Peter's Church, Budleigh Salterton.

Bob Grant

Bob Grant was born Robert St. Claire Grant on 14 April 1932, at 20, Rivercourt Road in Hammersmith, West London. Grant pursued his acting ambitions from an early age, and following his school years, and heavily influenced by his father, Albert George Grant, Bob joined RADA, funding his tuition with various jobs including a frozen food salesman and, ironically, a bus conductor.

In the early 1950s, Grant did his national service in the Royal Artillery at Kinmel Camp near Rhyl, North Wales. On demob, he made his stage début in Worm's Eye View at Court Royal, Horsham. Grant married on Jean Hyett 23 October 1954 at a Westcliffe-on-Sea church. The couple had a child together, Katherine.

Bob Grant's acting work was furthered with his first West End stage appearance in *The Good Soldier Schweik* in 1956. An accomplished writer, Bob also starred in his self-penned show, *Instant Marriage*, at the Piccadilly Theatre. A move to film came in 1963 when Grant appeared as Perce in the Theatre Workshop produced feature *Sparrows Can't Sing*.

Further theatre work including a stint in *Mrs Wilson's Diaries* with Stephen Lewis, brought Grant to the attention of *On the Buses* director Stuart Allen, who eventually cast the duo in the sitcom. But Albert Grant did not like his son's choice of lowbrow work. "Bob's father wasn't happy about him being in the show," Anna Karen explained. "I remember he said to him, 'All that money that I've spent on you, and you're a red-nosed clown.'"

Despite not pleasing his father's dreams of serious dramatics, Grant achieved stardom from *On the Buses*. Having been divorced before the sitcom, the show cost him his second wife, stage manager Christine Kemp, whom he married in

1962. They had had two children Robert and Charlotte. He had a short relationship with actress Gaye Brown before marrying ex-calendar girl Kim Benwell.

Bob married Kim on 31 October 1971 at Caxton Hall Register Office, Westminster, where crowds swarmed the streets outside to such an extent that the hired double decker bus due to be used to transport guests to the reception couldn't set off. The rest of the *On the Buses* cast attended the ceremony, but Bob's new wife wasn't incredibly popular among them. "Doris couldn't see why Bob left Gaye Brown," explained a friend of the actress. "She said to me how she didn't like Kim and that she had a 'bum-face'. It was hilarious the way she said it. That got me in trouble, as when I eventually met Kim I couldn't help but think of Doris's comments and laugh."

When *On the Buses* came to an end, Bob toured Australia in the farce *No Sex Please We're British*, and back in Britain *Stop it Nurse*, with Stephen Lewis and Anna Karen. In 1975 he wrote and appeared in a pilot for *Milk-O*, a comedy revolving around a milkman, which was broadcast on 26 November that year. "It was a *Comedy Premiere* in 1975 I think," Anna Karen remembers. "I was playing Bob's wife, and he was a milkman – the show was called *Milk-O*. Bob wrote it with Anthony Marriot."

Acting work started to dry up for Grant in the 1980s. He found it difficult to escape the clutches of typecasting, with casting directors viewing him as nothing more than a bus conductor. Some short runs in pantomimes followed, but steady work was impossible to find. In his *On the Buses* heyday, Bob had a Chelsea flat and a Rolls Royce car, by the 1980s he had to leave it behind and moved with wife Kim to a downsized life away from London.

Money worries caused by the lack of paid work led Grant into a deep depression, and eventually, in 1987, a suicide attempt. "I awoke in a horrible state," he explained in an interview after the event. "I just had to get out of the house. I left the house and thumbed a lift to Melton Mowbray, and then got a train to Birmingham New Street where I sat sobbing in a station buffet. Everyone ignored me. Normally I get asked in the street something like 'When you back on the telly then?' but not this time."

Bob started to write his first note to Kim, intending to have it sent to her after he had killed himself. "Tears streamed down my face as I wrote," Bob recalled. After hours pounding the streets of Birmingham, Grant instead caught the ferry to Dublin, "It was a horrible night on that boat," he continued. "I'd been to Dublin before and it seemed such a nice place. I wanted to end it all, either by jumping in the Liffey, or ironically throwing myself under a bus."

Bob stayed at a guesthouse in Dublin to think things over. He called Kim but there was no answer; she was, at the time, in London filming an appeal to find him. Grant eventually returned to England, where his absence had caused a small stir, leading him to garner a few more acting jobs. However, another gap in employment led to a second suicide attempt, this time by carbon monoxide poisoning in his car. Grant was discovered in time, and admitted to hospital for treatment.

Bob and Kim took a holiday to Goa in India to recover, and on their return it seemed things were finally going right again. Bob and Kim moved to a small cottage in Twyning, Gloucestershire with the ambition of making a fresh start. Regrettably, this didn't last as once more bills continued to arrive and work didn't. In despair, Bob Grant made a third and as it turned out final suicide attempt. This time he succeeded, dying in a fume-filled car on 8 November 2003, aged 71.

"I never knew Bob committed suicide," explained actress Ursula Mohan. "It was only when I did the *Comedy Classics* programme for ITV they told me and I was so shocked. He was a depressive but he always came across as so cheery. We'd always talk about the theatre and he was very well spoken. He wrote a lot and he was a very good actor – it's still sad thinking of his face and what happened to him."

Cast Appendix

Stephen Lewis

Stephen Lewis was born as Stephen Cato on 14 November 1936 in London. Beginning his career as a merchant seaman, he became a carpenter, working and living in Stratford, London. Living a short distance from the Joan Littlewood Theatre Workshop led Lewis to becoming a regular audience attendee, prior to getting to know the cast of the company socially, and as he explained in a 1971 interview, becoming "one of the family". "I'd stay after the show drinking until the early hours of the morning with actors like Bob Grant and Harry H. Corbett." Stephen continued.

His two worlds collided when Joan took the company down to Lewis's building yard where he was working. "They were putting on a play about builders and wanted the cast to get the feel of a builder's yard. That was it for me. I downed tools, went on the stage that week and I've been an actor ever since."

Stephen's fondness for the stage developed his writing talents, and whilst appearing in *The Hostage*, written by Brendan Behan, he began scripting a play of his own – one that turned into the iconic production *Sparrows Can't Sing*, which in 1962 became the first film to come from the theatre workshop. It starred Barbara Windsor and James Booth, together with the talents of Yootha Joyce, Brian Murphy, Roy Kinnear, Queenie Watts, Harry H. Corbett and Murray Melvin.

Back on the stage, Lewis took to the boards in *Mrs Wilson's Diary* – a show adapted for television by LWT and directed by Stuart Allen, the future director of *On the Buses*. Catching the eye of the producer, both Stephen Lewis, and his friend Bob Grant were selected as leads in the show in *On the Buses* in 1969.

Despite being only 33 at the time, Lewis made the martinet Blakey his own, and the role of the Inspector became his strongest and best-remembered part to date.

With his extensive writing talents and experience, Lewis and Grant continued writing *On the Buses* scripts for television when original series creators Ronald Wolfe and Ronald Chesney began to work on other projects, and even after the final series aired in 1973, the character of Blakey refused to die, and was reincarnated for the sequel, *Don't Drink the Water* which showed his character moving to Spain to retire away from the depot.

Sitcom work began to dry up for Lewis in the late 1970s; his previous work as a bus inspector typecast him, making it difficult for him to land other parts. Appearing on stage again with Bob Grant as well as Anna Karen in *Stop it Nurse* was a return to his *On the Buses* fame. Lewis was cast in cameo roles in the comedy sex films, *Adventures of a Taxi Driver* and *Adventures of a Plumber's Mate*, both under direction of Stanley Long.

In 1988, he was cast as Clem "Smiler" Hemmingway in Roy Clarke's *Last of the Summer Wine*, a role that would become Lewis's longest yet, continuing for a remarkable 20 years. Whilst the series wasn't in production, Lewis continued his acting in other comedies, notably a very Blakey-like Harry Lambert in *Oh Doctor Beeching*, and small parts in *One Foot in the Grave*, together with a cameo in an early episode of *Bodger and Badger*. Work finally finished for Stephen Lewis in 2007, when he missed filming *Last of the Summer Wine* due to health problems, and retired from the business.

Today, Stephen Lewis lives a reclusive life, having severed all ties with his former colleagues and acting friends. None of the writers or surviving cast of *On the Buses* are in touch with him. His last agent, Spotlight, claims to have no current details for him. Despite telling *TV Times* in 1971, "This is no longer just a job for me, I am dedicated to it, and I couldn't stop it," it looks like Blakey has finally hung up his mac.

Cast Appendix

<u>Anna Karen</u>

Anna Karen was born Anna McCall in Durban, South Africa, on 19 September 1936. "I was born in South Africa and moved to the UK at 17", she explained. "I'd always wanted to be an actress, I knew from when I was about seven and my first job was as the voice of a little mermaid in a production by the National Theatre".

On arrival in England, Karen immediately began chasing her dreams and enrolled in theatre school. "I went to the London School of Dramatic art, which was in Baker Street. I worked as a dishwasher in the hotel across the way to pay my tuition fees and rent."

But dishwashing soon lost its charm and Anna decided on another line of work. "I was a stripper," she laughed. "I got bored as a washer-upper, and I soon found you could make twice as much money. I then moved to Italy with my first husband for a while. We split up when we came back to England. I had, by this time, given up being an actress and I went back to stripping mainly because I was worried if I was legally in the UK, as South Africa had left the Commonwealth. I also did some work at Bertram Mills Circus, riding an elephant in the school holidays."

After a few months, the dreams of acting returned, and Anna decided to give stardom another shot. "I had learnt a lot about comedy from working at the Panama Club, I was working with Sid and Max Harrison and went on tour with them; that's also where I changed my name to Anna Karen. If you were foreign, you got £10 a week more – so I became Scandinavian!"

Eventually fame, be it in a dubious manner, came Karen's way, and she was cast in Arnold L. Miller's *Nudist Memories*. "I did that in 1961, and my first TV role was, I think, *The Eagle*

Rides the Tiger and then I was in *Poor Cow.*"

In 1969, Anna appeared in *Carry on Camping* alongside her friend Barbara Windsor. Later that year, she was chosen to become Olive in *On the Buses*, which remains her most famous role.

An attractive woman naturally, Karen was heavily made up to appear as the dowdy old frump, wearing padding and thick-rimmed glasses, which became the subject of multiple gags. She married Terry Duggan, an On the Buses support actor.

When *On the Buses* drew to an end, Karen returned to the stage with roles including *Stop it Nurse* with Bob Grant and Stephen Lewis at the Windmill Theatre. In 1977, she once again donned the mantle of Olive in the revival of Wolfe and Chesney's *The Rag Trade,* the series that made a star of her co-worker, Reg Varney, more than fifteen years earlier. She appeared alongside original series cast members Peter Jones and Miriam Karlin.

Anna continued television work through the 1980s appearing in *Troubles and Strife*, together with a regular role in *Roland Rat.* In reality, Anna herself became a rat, albeit a water one. She has long been a supporter of the charity organisation the Grand Order of the Water Rats for many years and became Queen Ratling in 1990. In 1996, she took a small part in *EastEnders*, reuniting with Barbara Windsor to play her on-screen sister, Sal Martin.

Today, Anna remains a familiar face onscreen. She appeared on *The Sunday Night Project* and was a talking head for *Piers Morgan's Life Stories* when the former *Daily Mirror* editor interviewed Barbara Windsor. Anna's husband Terry Duggan sadly passed away on 1 May 2008. Anna currently lives in Ilford, Essex.

Michael Robbins

Michael Anthony Robbins was born on 14 November 1930, and prior to acting, worked as a bank clerk in his hometown of Hitchin, Hertfordshire. An unfortunate incident with a fire extinguisher resulted in Michael losing his telling job and he moved on to join local amateur dramatics societies. He appeared in various stage roles and made his television début in Be Soon in 1957. Further parts soon followed with *Roll on Bloomin' Death, Crane, Suspense, Ghost Squad*, and *Diary of a Young Man.*

Robbins was also a student at Birmingham Rep, where he met his future wife, actress Hal Dyer. "I did a Christmas show with him called *The Silver Curlew*," Hal recalls. "I had to teach him how to dance. I did three years in Birmingham, and then Michael left to go to London. We didn't see much of each other at first."

Michael also took film parts, acting with Stephen Lewis in *A Prize of Arms* starring Stanley Baker. Robbins developed his comedic talents appearing in shows with comics Frankie Howerd, Dick Emery, and Harry Worth — with the latter bringing him to the attention of writers Ronald Wolfe and Ronald Chesney and leading to his casting in *On the Buses*.

Robbins stayed with *On the Buses* for six series, before leaving the sitcom to return to theatre, appearing with Tom Courtenay in London's West End.

"Michael always preferred television work," his widow Hal Dyer recalled. "It was better money, but he enjoyed it a lot. He was the only actor in *On the Buses,* as in the old genre of the actor. He had done all the previous theatre and rep work, whereas most of the others had come from variety".

When the production ended, Robbins took a series stint as Eddie Cropper in *How's Your Father,* prior to appearing in the film version of *Man About the House* and working with Peter Sellers in *The Pink Panther Strikes Again*. Robbins continued acting up to the year of his death in 1992, with his last credited role as an irate neighbour in *One Foot in the Grave.*

Michael's capitalised on his fame for charity, raising vast amounts for various good causes and working as a volunteer for various societies. He was a member of the Grand Order of Water Rats, and in 1978 was elected Rat of the Year. "He was frequently recognised out and about, even abroad," Dyer explained. "*On the Buses* was huge in Holland and Australia. There was a huge following for it and most British comedy."

Michael Robbins cut back on his television work in the late 1980s, appearing in *Hi-De-Hi* and *EastEnders* prior to his last credited role in *One Foot in the Grave*. He died of cancer in Caterham, Surrey on 11 December 1992.

Cast Appendix

<u>Doris Hare</u>

Doris Hare was born in Bargoed, Wales on 1 March 1905. Her first stage role was at the tender age of three, in *Current Cash*, a show performed in her parents' mobile theatre, which travelled around South Wales. Coming from a theatrical family she was in many shows before taking a solo dive to tread the boards on her own as 'Little Doris Hare'.

Hare toured in dozens of theatres, variety shows and music halls around the region, gradually moving in to mainstream theatre and starring in plays by Alan Bennett, Harold Pinter and George Bernard Shaw. She even had a play written especially for her by Noël Coward.

In 1930, Hare toured in *The Show's The Thing* and afterwards moved onto radio shows at BBC Savoy Hill. In the late 1930s she began appearing in films with *Night Mail* (1934), *Opening Night* (1935) and *Jubilee Window* (1935) her first screen appearances. Hare also took part in *Shipmates Ashore*, which was put together for the Merchant Navy – it was this role that earned Doris the MBE in 1941.

After several more film parts, Hare made her television début in 1953 in *Douglas Fairbanks Jr Presents*. After a string of appearances on the small screen, she returned to her theatrical roots and in the 1960s, spent a year with the National Theatre, three years with the Royal Shakespeare and several seasons at the Chichester Festival Theatre.

Doris was cast in *On the Buses* in 1969, taking over from Cicely Courtneidge from the second series onwards. "I got on very well with Doris," explained actress Ursula Mohan. "I adored her, she had these superb stories about Noël Coward and her incredible upbringing. All her sisters were in theatre and were called the Little Hares."

When *On the Buses* came to an end, Doris Hare went back

to theatres as well as continuing her television work in *Nanny, Never the Twain, Diamonds* and *Sharing Time*. In 1982 she won a Variety Club award for her contributions to show business.

Hare continued in films, theatre and television up until the late 1990s, her last film being *Nuns on the Run*.

She returned to stage in the farce *It Runs In The Family* and finally at the London Palladium for one night in a tribute to Evelyn Laye.

In late 1998, Doris took up residency at the actors' retirement home, Denville Hall in Middlesex, where she died on 30 May 2000, aged 95.

Bibliography

Further Reading:

Writing Comedy - Ronald Wolfe
Robert Hale Ltd 2003 - ISBN: 978-0709074137

My Life in Memoirs - Ronald Wolfe
Kaleidoscope Publishing 2010 - ISBN: 978-1900203388

The Little Clown - Reg Varney
Hodder and Stoughton 1990 - ISBN: 978-0340520772

By the same author:

Man About the House - George and Mildred : The Definitive
Companion - Tex Fisher
Deck Chair Publishing 2010 - ISBN: 978-0956563408

Clippies turned writers

Brotherhood of Blades - Linda Regan
Creme de la Crime Books 2011 - ISBN: 978-1780290096

Behind You! / Dead Like Her / Passion Killers - Linda Regan
Creme de la Crime books 2006 - 2009

Down a Tuscan Alley - Laura Graham
Solstice Publishing 2011 - ISBN: N/A

Notes:

Coming to bed now, Arthur?